CW00967819

SAMS
Teach Yourself
UNIX®

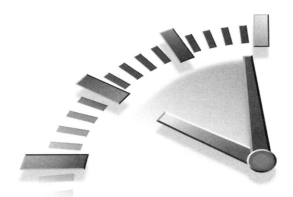

William Ray

in 10 Minutes

SAMS

201 West 103rd St., Indianapolis, Indiana, 46290 USA

International Standard Book Number: 0-672-31523-8

Library of Congress Catalog Card Number: 98-89638

Printed in the United States of America

First Printing: February, 1999

05   04   03   02   8   7   6   5

TRADEMARKS

WARNING AND DISCLAIMER

Executive Editor
Grace Buechlein

Development Editor
Laura Bulcher

Managing Editor
Brice Gosnell

Project Editor
Natalie F. Harris

Copy Editor
JoAnna Kremer

Indexer
Erika Millen

Proofreaders
Andrew Beaster
Benjamin Berg
Billy Fields

Technical Editor
Aron Hsiao
Eric Richardson

Interior Design
Gary Adair

Cover Design
Aren Howell

Layout Technicians
Brandon Allen
Stacey DeRome
Timothy Osborn
Amy Parker
Staci Somers

CONTENTS

PART IV WORKING WITH THE SHELL

11 PROCESSES   112

12 INPUT AND OUTPUT   125

13 REGULAR EXPRESSIONS   131

14 BASIC SHELL SCRIPTING   137

PART VII ADVANCED TOPICS

ABOUT THE AUTHOR

William Ray is a UNIX system administrator, programmer and trainer.
After acquiring a B.S. in Mathematics and an M.S. in Computer Science,
Will spent five years getting paid to have fun—as a programmer building
X Window System user interfaces. For the past six years, he has been
perpetually two years away from attaining his Ph.D. in Biophysics. To
maintain his sanity while arguing with test-tubes and microbes, Will
developed a computer-graphics center for The Ohio State University's
College of Biological Sciences. Supporting an assortment of Silicon
Graphics and Sun UNIX hardware, Will has been the center's system
administrator, Webmaster, and acting director. He also has provided user
support and UNIX training for several hundred students and faculty members who have come to use the center.

In a recent attempt to shorten the two-year graduation horizon, Will
trained his wife to take over the center's administration. While this seems
to have shortened the graduation timeframe, he appears to be incapable of
keeping his nose out of computer topics. So, he has been distracting himself by writing computer texts and pestering his wife about the center.

DEDICATION

To my dear wife, Joan, for being my most apt UNIX pupil.

ACKNOWLEDGMENTS

Thanks to everyone who helped with this project. I would like to especially thank my brother, John, for his collaborative work, and my wife, Joan, for correcting my atrocious grammar and putting up with my odd writing hours. I would also like to thank my Development Editor, Laura Bulcher, and my Executive Editor, Grace Buechlein, for disproving everything I've heard about editors; and the technical editors, Aron Hsiao and Eric Richardson, for keeping me honest.

TELL US WHAT YOU THINK!

As the reader of this book, *you* are our most important critic and commentator. We value your opinion and want to know what we're doing right, what we could do better, what areas you'd like to see us publish in, and any other words of wisdom you're willing to pass our way.

I welcome your comments. You can email or write me directly to let me know what you did or didn't like about this book—as well as what we can do to make our books stronger.

Please note that I cannot help you with technical problems related to the topic of this book, and that due to the high volume of mail I receive, I might not be able to reply to every message.

When you write, please be sure to include this book's title and author as well as your name and phone or fax number. I will carefully review your comments and share them with the author and editors who worked on the book.

E-mail: feedback@samspublishing.com

Mail: Mark Taber
            Associate Publisher
            Sams Publishing
            201 West 103rd Street
            Indianapolis, IN 46290 USA

INTRODUCTION

WELCOME TO THE WORLD OF UNIX

Welcome to *Sam's Teach Yourself UNIX in 10 Minutes*. If you're like most individuals faced with using UNIX for the first time, there are probably a dozen notions you have about what using UNIX will be like—mostly all of them intimidating. People have probably told you that UNIX is difficult to use, that the commands are cryptic, and that the interface is non-intuitive. You've almost certainly heard that UNIX is powerful, but that the power comes at the price of a steep learning curve. The thought that learning and using UNIX will be fun and rewarding is probably one of the furthest from your mind. The contents of this book will hopefully change your mind. You will learn how to make use of UNIX's command line and graphical user interface, and to familiarize yourself with the commands you need to productively use UNIX on a day-to-day basis.

SO WHAT IS UNIX, ANYWAY?

UNIX is a powerful multitasking (it can run multiple programs simultaneously) operating system. Having been designed originally as an experimental operating system on which to test OS implementation ideas, UNIX grew from its humble roots to the leading commercial platform for network server and program development.

Because of its roots, many parts of UNIX are implemented in what might be considered "the easiest way possible." Although this leads to certain inefficiencies in the OS, it also proves to be one of UNIX's greatest strengths—many of the "easiest way possible" ideas turn out to be great benefits to the user. The easiest way possible tends, for example, to lead to abstraction of where data is stored or how it is accessed. Rather than being concerned where something is located, it's easier to design a single way of accessing data. Then whenever data needs to be retrieved from some new type of device, you create a piece of software that allows the new data to be accessed through the pre-existing interface.

UNIX is also a multi-user operating system. Unlike some personal-computer implementations of the idea of multiple users, with UNIX, many users can simultaneously use a single machine. From the point of view of each of these users, they are in control of the complete machine. Also, instead of simply hiding your files from other users UNIX actually gives you the capability to deny or allow other users access to your files, making them invisible—and inaccessible to users who are denied access.

One of the interesting things you'll discover about UNIX after you've used it for a while is that many of the more useful utilities and applications are written by, and supported by, other users just like yourself. The power of the UNIX operating system, the ease with which sophisticated commands can be constructed, and UNIX's powerful programming and networking ties have bred a strong cooperative streak in UNIX users. It is a long-standing tradition that software constructed to solve a problem is made available by its author to the rest of the UNIX community, and this becomes yet another building block for even more sophisticated commands. You might be surprised to find that the most powerful compiler and debuggers available for UNIX are available for free, as are many other useful applications. Although you might be familiar with the idea of *shareware* from the personal computer world, the idea of UNIX *freeware* is likely to take you at least slightly by surprise. Much of the UNIX freeware rivals or surpasses commercial software in its elegance, completeness, and—most of all—in the rapidity of response to the report of errors in the software. Unlike singular shareware authors, much UNIX freeware is supported by entire user communities. For example, if you're using one of the freeware UNIX database systems and discover a bug, it would not be unexpected for one of the hundreds of users who contribute code to that particular project to have your bug fixed—and a new version released in less than a week.

VERSIONS OF UNIX

With only a little looking around, you're likely to notice that there are many different versions (frequently called *flavors*) of UNIX available, sometimes even coming in multiple flavors from a single vendor. The largest consistent difference you will notice if you use multiple different versions of UNIX is between versions based on AT&T's *System V* UNIX and the Berkeley Standard Distribution *BSD4.X* UNIX. This book has been written to be as general as possible and to not favor any one vendor or implementation. Where variations between command behavior is known to the author it has been noted in the text, but there certainly is the possibility (probability? certainty?—yes, certainty) that there are other variations as well. This book will teach you how to use UNIX's built-in manuals and help system to find additional information on commands that do not function as described here.

 Tip If something in an example doesn't work on your system, don't be alarmed—check the online manuals or ask other users of your machine. Different versions of UNIX sometimes have slightly different versions of commands—it will be worth your time to learn how things work on your system.

HOW DO YOU USE UNIX?

Unless you're simply using a UNIX machine as a platform for a prepackaged commercial application, most of your interaction with UNIX is likely to be textual—commands typed at a command-line prompt. Most implementations of UNIX do provide a *GUI* (*graphical user interface*); however, even when running the GUI, much of what you are likely to do involves typing commands into *terminal windows* which are available in the GUI.

Don't let the fact that you have to use textual commands worry you. Although it's not as intuitively obvious as dragging and dropping to copy files, the command-line interface is actually one of UNIX's strengths. Again doing things the easy way, UNIX commands tend to be simple commands that do one simple thing. It is the capability to combine many of these simple commands together to make much more complex commands—commands suited to do almost anything you can imagine—which makes UNIX truly powerful.

On some versions of UNIX you might also find useful utilities built-in as part of the GUI. Some of these make the GUI almost as sophisticated as the personal computer interfaces with which you might be familiar. You will be introduced to *KDE* (*K Desktop Environment*), one particular flavor of such an interface, in this book. KDE was chosen as a representative sample for this book because it is available on a wide range of UNIX flavors, because it is one of the more sophisticated examples, and because it is a wonderful example of a free product supported by its users.

Word of Caution   As tempting as it might be, you are cautioned not to become entirely dependent on GUI utilities even if you have a GUI product with the sophistication and convenience of KDE. Although the GUI utilities are often faster and much easier than using the command line, it is rare for a GUI version of a command to have the same power and extensibility that the command line version will have. If you rely only on the GUI, you will be limiting yourself and not making use of the full power you have at your disposal.

HOW TO USE THIS BOOK

This book is designed as a series of lessons. The earlier lessons give you an overview of how to start using UNIX, how to get help, and a bit of the UNIX philosophy to help you to understand why some things have been done in the way that they have. The lessons progress through examples of the sorts of commands you'll need to use the very first time you sit down at the machine, through more advanced topics. For the early topics you will find line-by-line instructions on the use of most commands, with examples that you can follow at your own machine. As the topics become more advanced, the information becomes more of an overview of the functionality of the commands. When you've reached that point, don't hesitate to use UNIX's built-in manuals. With the immense number of commands and diverse functionality available to the UNIX user, it is impossible to cover even a small fraction of the commands in-depth in a book this size. Instead, you are provided with the resources to find the in-depth information, and sufficient information to know what you need to be looking for.

If you're completely new to UNIX, it's recommended that you start at the beginning, and work your way through at least Lesson 7, "Reading Files." By the time you've completed Lesson 7, you will have mastered enough UNIX commands to give you an idea of what UNIX is all about and to let you start being productive with UNIX. You are, of course, encouraged to continue with the rest of the lessons. If you have a particular task in mind after you've completed Lesson 7, you will be ready to pick and choose what you need to know from the remaining lessons.

If you already have some familiarity with UNIX, but are looking for a quick-start on some more advanced topics, feel free to pick through the lessons for the portions about which you want to learn. No examples in the book rely on the results of previous examples, so you can step in anywhere you want. If your UNIX experience is such that you're comfortable moving around, and perhaps executing a few programs, you might feel ready to tackle some of the more advanced topics right off. You're encouraged to at least skim through the introductory lessons anyway, as you might not have been exposed to some of the "philosophy" of UNIX yet. This can be helpful in understanding the how and why of some of the more sophisticated lessons.

WHO THIS BOOK IS FOR

This book is aimed primarily at the user coming to UNIX for the first time, or with very little UNIX experience, who wants or needs to become a productive UNIX user without a large investment of time. The lessons are styled, and commands and options presented, in such a way that the new user can quickly start to use UNIX without needing to grasp all the intricacies of each and every command. In addition to the most common commands and command options, the user is given the capability to find more information as his or her needs grow. In the more advanced lessons, the user is presented with an overview that is sufficient to demonstrate the possibilities and capabilities inherent in the UNIX environment, and with the tools to begin to take advantage of those capabilities.

Users who have used UNIX for some time—but only casually—who find that they want to learn more or to be more comfortable with UNIX will also benefit from this book, both as a quick reference and as a stepping stone to greater understanding and fluency with the OS.

A QUICK NOTE FROM THE AUTHOR

Don't let UNIX intimidate you—whether you're here for work or for pleasure, don't let your UNIX experience frustrate you. Having been using UNIX and training others to use UNIX since 1989, the single largest problem that I see new users experience is that they allow using UNIX to *become* work, rather than making UNIX work for them.

UNIX is a very powerful operating system that will enable you to customize it to suit your personal wants and needs, and this book will show you how to make it work for you. In years of training users to use UNIX machines for a computer graphics lab, I have seen far too many users refuse to actually learn how to make their machines work for them. Instead of investing a few minutes in learning how to customize the OS and environment to make their lives easier, they spend hours or days plodding through repetitive tasks by hand. You can make your life easier, your work go faster, and your computer experience much more pleasant if you think of UNIX as a box of parts which you can put together to create any tool you want. Singly, none of the parts is particularly interesting or powerful, but by correctly assembling these parts, a clever user can make UNIX do almost all his or her work automatically.

Read the book, work through any examples you need, but most importantly, remember that what is contained here is only a teaser of what can really be done with UNIX.

CONVENTIONS USED IN THIS BOOK

This book uses the following conventions:

- Information you type appears in **`bold monospace`** type.

- Screen output will be shown in `monospace`.

- Menus and menu options, keys you press, and names of buttons and other screen components with which you might interact appear in **bolded blue type**.

- The **Return** key is synonymous with the **Enter** key.

In addition, this book uses the following sidebars to identify helpful information:

 Tips lead you to shortcuts and solutions that can clear up confusion or save you time.

 Cautions help you avoid common pitfalls.

 Plain English explains new terms and definitions.

LESSON 1
GETTING STARTED

In this lesson you'll learn about logging in to and out of your UNIX system in addition to some basics of operating your machine. You'll also learn a bit of the UNIX background, such as why it runs the way it does.

For years UNIX has been a murky topic that has scared away many people. The Internet and World Wide Web were built upon the backs of UNIX machines; therefore, the growing need for Internet connectivity, combined with a desire for increased performance and stability, have caused the number of people interested in using UNIX to skyrocket. At the same time, personal computers are becoming easier to use, and this has spurred the growth of utilities to make the UNIX user's life easier. Furthermore, this has aided in the push of UNIX—in all its variants—from the server room onto the desktop and into the home.

THE LOGIN PROCESS

The first thing you'll notice when you sit down in front of your UNIX computer is that you need to log in before you can do anything. UNIX is based on a *multi-user* principle—multiple users can have their own accounts, programs, and settings on the same machine. If you're familiar with Windows 95/98, multiple users might sound familiar. Windows 95/98 however, does not protect the user's files from other people; it simply "hides" them. Furthermore, Windows 95/98 does not enable multiple users to run programs simultaneously the way UNIX does.

OWNERSHIP AND PERMISSIONS

UNIX contains the concepts of *ownership* and *permissions*. Files are owned by individual users, and permissions control who can view, edit, or run files on the system. Luckily, there is little need for a casual user to worry about ownership. If there is a need to share files with other users on the system, you'll want to take a look at Lesson 19, "Permissions." After you've logged in to your computer, all files that you create during your current session are automatically owned by your account.

MULTI-USER

In addition to controlling and tracking who owns what, UNIX also enables multiple users to access the system simultaneously. This is a drastic change from the desktop environment offered by traditional personal computer operating systems. For example, while you're working on a spreadsheet, a coworker might be running a series of calculations for an engineering project. Many different processes can run simultaneously on a single computer by potentially hundreds of different users. Lesson 11, "Processes" explains the concept of processes and how you can manage them.

THE login PROMPT

In order to log in to your computer, you need to supply a username and password. Your system administrator will most likely provide you with a username and password. Upon entering your information, UNIX loads the appropriate configuration for your account and you can start using the system. The screen that is displayed when you enter your username and password varies from system to system depending on the configuration. There are two possibilities that you might encounter: a graphical login screen or a text-based screen.

 To Shift or Not to Shift   When you're logging in to— or using other aspects of—UNIX, it's important to remember that UNIX is case-sensitive. The operating system interprets the capital and lowercase forms of a letter as two different characters. So, if you've been given a password that looks like KiWisRgood, you can bet that the machine won't allow you to log in with kiwisrgood.

TEXT-BASED LOGIN

The text-based login screen varies by UNIX distributions. Most text-based UNIX login prompts look like this:

```
login:
password:
```

When you see the `login:` prompt, type your username and press return. The `password:` prompt appears immediately thereafter. When you have successfully typed in both your username and password, you reach a shell prompt. There are a couple of things to keep in mind during your login: Don't backspace because some systems don't interpret it properly. Also, when you type your password the data won't show on the screen (this is to protect your account from prying eyes). Now you're ready to begin issuing commands to the system. Don't worry if you don't know what to do next; you'll soon learn how to do something productive.

 What if I Make a Typing Error? Don't worry if you make a mistake logging in. The system logs the failed attempt to a security file. In the default UNIX configuration, you have another chance to log in, so there's no need to panic if you don't get it right the first time—everyone makes mistakes!

GRAPHICAL LOGIN

Instead of a text prompt, your machine might be configured with something a bit snazzier—a graphical screen where you can type your login information. This works exactly the same as the text-based system, except it immediately launches you into the X Windows environment. Some of these graphical login screens enable the user to select from various login shells or to perform certain administrative tasks, but all provide the basic utility of logging in to the system. They each have an area for you to enter your username and an area for you to enter your password. Some flavors of UNIX enable you to **tab** between these fields, whereas other variations require you to position your cursor over each field and click to select the field in which you want to type. In any case, enter your username and password in the obvious locations, and then either hit **return** or click on the **login** button.

THE LOGOUT PROCESS

Now that you know how to log in to your system, here's a quick look at the logout process and why it is important. You already know that your computer can have multiple people using it simultaneously, and that it can have files owned by many different people. The login process identifies you to the system and enables you to control the computer using your own username. How do you reverse this? That's where the logout process fits. It closes any files that you might have open and shuts down any programs that you might have left running. If you remain logged in constantly, you might be exposing the system to security risks—not to mention that the processes you leave running might slow down the computer for other users. It's always best to log out of your computer when you're finished using it. UNIX users might encounter serious troubles when they don't properly log out.

LOGGING OUT FROM A TEXT-BASED SESSION

If you are not running a graphical session (you don't see any windows on your screen), the only command you need to use to log out is logout, surprisingly enough.

In order to log out from a command prompt, type:

```
>logout
```

The system immediately returns to the login prompt. That's it. You've successfully logged out of the computer.

Logout Alternative   Some UNIX shells have the reputation of being picky. In certain cases, when you type **logout** the UNIX shell might reply with the message "Not login shell" and proceed to leave you logged in. Not to worry—even if a shell refuses to accept the logout command, you can still log out with the exit command. It works the same way as logout and will convince even picky versions of UNIX to allow you to sign off of the system.

LOGGING OUT FROM A KDE SESSION

If you logged in to the UNIX system through the KDE graphical interface, you can point and click your way out of the system. To log out:

1. Click the **K** symbol, which pops up the main KDE menu.

2. Select **Logout** from the menu

3. KDE prompts you and tells you that it is ready to close your session. Click the **Logout** button to complete the process.

THE UNIX COMMAND PROMPT

You're probably wondering what use UNIX is going to be to you if all
you can do is log in and log out. Patience! UNIX can be a bit overwhelming if approached too quickly. The power of UNIX comes from its wealth
of built-in utilities and the way that processes can be combined to perform
tasks that might require customized programming on another operating
system. For example, suppose you're running a Web server on your UNIX
computer and you want to count the number of accesses from a machine
named *kiwi*. If you're a programmer, it isn't too difficult to write a program to do this—but with UNIX you don't need to! Instead, you can just
enter a command such as this:

```
>grep "kiwi" /var/log/httpd/access.log ¦ wc -l
```

This example uses grep, a program that finds patterns, to find all the lines
in the Web server log which contain *kiwi*; it then hands the results to wc, a
program which counts things. Obviously, you aren't expected to know
how to construct this command yet—but you will be capable of doing so
by the end of the book.

When you are typing commands into UNIX, you are typing them into
what is known as a shell. For all the old DOS users out there, a shell is
sort of like a version of Command.Com—on steroids. If you remember the
days of DOS, you probably also remember different DOS shells that
added capabilities to your computer. UNIX has a wide variety of shells
that you can use, each offering a different set of capabilities. In addition
to giving the user a place to run commands, shells also provide a scripting
language that is much like a DOS batch file, but far more capable.
Programs written using a shell are called *shell scripts*.

LOTS AND LOTS OF SHELLS

Because there are numerous shells available for UNIX, most users try different shells until they find the one that they like best. You'll probably never need to change your shell unless you plan on programming one. Lesson 15, "User Utilities," discusses the techniques you can use to switch to a different shell. Here is a quick overview of just a few of the different shells that are available, and the benefits they offer:

- **sh**—The Bourne shell, sh is *the* shell; it is available on any UNIX distribution that you might use, and it offers a simple scripting syntax. Most people use the sh shell only when they are writing programs that must run on absolutely any UNIX machine.

- **csh**—The C-Shell. (Yes, it's pronounced like *seashell*.) The csh shell takes its name from the C programming language. The scripting environment that is offered by csh is similar to the C language and offers enough flexibility to write lengthy, customized scripts that run on most UNIX machines.

- **tcsh**—Extended C-shell. This shell is csh with various extensions, and it's a very popular alternative to csh on most UNIX variations. This shell includes filename completion and an easily accessible command history.

- **bash**—The Bourne-again shell. (UNIX programmers have been known to have weird senses of humor.) bash is a modern shell that has received most of its attention from the Linux community and is included as the default shell on most Linux machines. This shell has the same capabilities of csh but offers advanced features for the user as well as the programmer. bash includes command and filename completion and an easily accessible command history that is persistent across different login sessions.

There are far more shells available, but these four will probably make up the bulk of any that you encounter. Don't worry if you sit down in front of a computer that is running a different shell. You can still operate the computer using the knowledge gained from this book. You might experience some differences in the scripting architecture, but you're not going to be lost.

SHELL COMMAND SYNTAX

Using a shell is as simple as typing the command you want to use and pressing enter. There are a few rules, however, that might help if you are having trouble getting a command to work:

- Commands are case-sensitive, and are usually lowercase. Unlike Windows, you cannot mix case and still have a function work; you must type the command exactly as it is stored on the system.

- Frequently, the current directory isn't included in the PATH environment variable that specifies all the directories of the commands that you can access by typing just the command's name. (You'll find out how to modify this in Lesson 16, "Modifying the User Environment.") Because the current directory isn't necessarily included, you might be in a directory that holds a program called *parachute* but you'll find that you can't run the program by typing **parachute.** In order to run the command, simply tell the system that the parachute command is in the same directory that you are in by preceding it with ./. Thus, parachute can be run by typing ./**parachute** from inside its directory.

 What's with the . and /? These characters represent the current directory (.) and the directory separator (/). Used together, ./ is essentially the path to the directory that you are currently in.

- There are special symbols, commands, and so on, that might leave your shell in a state that seems unusable. This generally means that you've started some sort of process that is expecting input from you. There are three control characters that might help you regain control of your commands. To type one of these control characters, hold down the control key while pressing the corresponding letter:

  - **Ctrl+d**—Tells the computer that you are done sending input to a command. This is useful if you've accidentally started a program and can't get out.

- **Ctrl+c**—The UNIX break character. This usually kills any program that is currently running, and then returns you to a command prompt.

- **Ctrl+z**—Suspends the current process. This suspends the process you were running and returns you to a command prompt. Logging out kills the suspended command.

Don't be afraid to try the commands discussed in the book, and to explore the system to find more. You'll be amazed at what can be done with a little bit of typing.

SUMMARY

This lesson taught you a few very important skills that you need to begin using your UNIX computer effectively. Although most of the concepts introduced are relatively simple, they are important in understanding how and why UNIX operates the way it does.

- **Login**—Logging in to UNIX allows the system to identify you as a user and apply the appropriate ownership to files you create and modify. Each user has his or her own environment and can run programs simultaneously with other users.

- **Logout**—Logging out of the computer closes open files and ends processes that are owned by the current user. Always log out of the system when you are done using it.

- **The Command Line**—The UNIX command line enables you to create complex functions by stringing together a variety of built-in commands. What requires specialized software on other systems can usually be accomplished using built-in UNIX utilities.

- **Shells**—There are many different types of shells that you can use. Depending on your needs as a programmer and user, you need to evaluate the shell features you find necessary, and choose appropriately.

- **Using the Command Line**—Commands can be typed directly into a shell, as you might expect. Keep in mind that commands are usually lowercase, and you might need to specify a path to a command if it is not included in your PATH environment variable.

LESSON 2

UNIX DOCUMENTATION AND FINDING HELP

This lesson will show you how to find help using several methods of retrieving information about UNIX's built-in commands and capabilities.

If you've poked around your UNIX system at all, you've probably noticed that there are literally thousands of different files and applications on your computer. You might find this to be a bit overwhelming at first, but the diversity and extensive capabilities of the operating system are part of its attraction. If there is something you want to do, you can bet that UNIX has a utility or combination of utilities that can get the job done. The biggest question on your mind is probably, "How do I use this stuff?"

UNIX MANUAL PAGES

Although some UNIX commands provide instant feedback and help information to you if you simply type the command on the command line, this help is usually only useful for the experienced user who just needs a quick reminder. The UNIX *manual (man) pages*, on the other hand, are the quickest and easiest source for complete information on how to use the commands on your system. They provide information on what programs do and how to use them, as well as on other related utilities that you might be interested in checking out. If you're a programmer, man pages can also provide useful programming information.

man

To display a manual page, use the man command. In its simplest form, you can use man followed by the command you want to look up.

For example, to look up the man page for the date command:

```
>man date

DATE(1)
DATE(1)

NAME
        date - print or set the system date and time

SYNOPSIS
        date  [-u] [-d datestr] [-s datestr] [--utc]
        [--universal] [--date=datestr] [--set=datestr]
        [--help] [--version] [+FORMAT] [MMDDhhmm[[CC]YY][.ss]]

DESCRIPTION
        This manual page documents the GNU version of date.
        date with no arguments prints the current time and date
        (in the format  of  the `%c' directive described below).
        If given an argument that starts with a `+', it prints
        the  current time  and  date  in  a format controlled by
        that argument, which has the same format as the format
        string  passed  to the `strftime' function.
...
```

Turn Off the Alarm   Don't be alarmed if your system returns information which differs from what is shown here in response to man date. Different manufacturers—and different versions of UNIX—sometimes provide slightly different commands, and the man pages you see reflect the correct information for your system.

If your man command returns with no information, a complaint that it can't find the man page for date, or—worse yet—the dreaded command not found response, contact your system administrator. You might be stuck on a machine with missing or broken man pages, and your administrator can most likely fix it for you.

How do I Read the Rest?   When you see a . . . on your screen, there's more text to be read. The man pages won't scroll automatically, so you'll need to press the **Spacebar** to see additional text. Press **q** to quit the page and return to the command line.

This is only a tiny subset of the information that is returned via the man command, but enough for you to get the picture. You'll soon find that using man pages to learn about everything that is available on your system is going to take a bit of time. You can speed things up by viewing a summary description of a command through one of four different commands: man -f, man -k, whatis, or apropos, followed by the name of the command you'd like to explore. Each of these functions returns similar results, but there are two different ways that the search is performed.

man VARIATIONS, apropos, whatis

If you know the command you'd like to look up, use man -f, or **whatis**, followed by the command name.

For example, to print a summary for the date command, type:

```
>man -f date
date (1)              - print or set the system date and time
END
```

A short description of what date does is returned. Press **q** to return to the command line.

If you're not quite sure what you're looking for, man -f and whatis search the description of each available command for matching keywords. If you experience any errors while running these commands it might be because the whatis database has been removed from your system, or has not been created. You'll need to contact your system administrator and ask her or him to use makewhatis to generate the database files necessary to use whatis. Because this is a function that affects protected areas of the system, it is not available to most users.

Now, try running **whatis** on the subject **time**. This turns up several relevant entries.

```
>whatis time
time (2)              - get time in seconds
time (n)             - Time the execution of a script
Time::Local (3)      - efficiently compute time from local and
                       GMT time
Time::gmtime (3)     - by-name interface to Perl's built-in
                       gmtime() function
Time::localtime (3)  - by-name interface to Perl's built-in
                       localtime() function
Time::tm (3)         - internal object used by Time::gmtime and
                       Time::localtime
END
```

You can see that the time keyword has turned up six different entries in the whatis database. To return to the command prompt, you'll need to press **q**.

What do the Extra Letters and Numbers Mean?
You've probably noticed that some commands are followed by a letter or numeral; this is the section number for that command. For instance, time is followed by both n and 2. This means that there are two separate uses for the time command. To learn information about each of the variations, use man followed by the section number or letter and the command. For example, man n time or man 2 time.

If you're entirely unsure of what you want and a keyword search does not return anything useful, try the **apropos** or **man -k** command. This searches the descriptions much like whatis does, but also displays partial matches to the string you specify.

Try running **apropos** on **time** and compare your results with the results from the similar **whatis time** command:

```
>apropos time
clock (3)            - Determine processor time
clock (n)            - Obtain and manipulate time
convdate (1)         - convert time/date strings and numbers
date (1)             - print or set the system date and time
difftime (3)         - calculate time difference
```

```
ftime (3)          - return date and time
ftpshut (8)        - close down the ftp servers at a given
                     time
kbdrate (8)        - reset the keyboard repeat rate and delay
                     time
ldconfig (8)       - determine run-time link bindings
metamail (1)       - infrastructure for mailcap-based
                     multimedia mail handling
nanosleep (2)      - pause execution for a specified time
nwfstime (1)       - Display / Set a NetWare server's date
                     and time
parsedate (3)      - convert time and date string to number
...
```

This command actually turned up more than 70 matches on my system, far more than whatis time displayed. Try to be as specific as possible when you use apropos or man -k, or you might spend a great deal of time wading through extraneous information. Don't forget, the ... means there's more information to be accessed by pressing the spacebar. As before, pressing **q** returns you to the command prompt.

BUILT-IN HELP

Many of the common UNIX commands have a built-in help that isn't as verbose as the man pages—and it can be brought up in a jiffy. If you find that you're constantly using the man pages to find the options that are available for a specific command, you might want to see if it has its own help summary page. If you've spent much time using the compression or archiving utilities, you'll know what I mean. For many commands --help provides the information you need. In some cases, it might be as simple as -h or -?. If the first one doesn't work, try again. It's quite possible that built-in help is not available, so don't be surprised if you run into cases where this doesn't work as you had hoped.

To view the built-in help for the date command, type:

```
>date --help
Usage: date [OPTION]... [+FORMAT]
  or:  date [OPTION] [MMDDhhmm[[CC]YY][.ss]]
Display the current time in the given FORMAT, or set the system
date.

  -d, --date=STRING        display time described by STRING,
```

```
                             not `now'
-f, --file=DATEFILE          like --date once for each line of
                             DATEFILE
-r, --reference=FILE         display the last modification time
                             of FILE
-R, --rfc-822                output RFC-822 compliant date string
-s, --set=STRING             set time described by STRING
-u, --utc, --universal       print or set Coordinated Universal
                             Time
    --help                   display this help and exit
    --version                output version information and exit
...
```

Although not as descriptive as the man pages, the information is useful and to the point.

Depending on the resources that are available, your system administrator might have chosen to forgo the installation of man pages on your UNIX system. The amount of disk space used by the manual pages is not trivial, and in these cases you'll learn to appreciate the built-in help feature provided by many applications.

Additional Documentation

Many pieces of software install additional documentation into a special info database that can be accessed via the emacs editor's **Meta-X-info** command. In the emacs editor, which is covered more completely in Lesson 8, "Text Editing," you can enter the info database by typing (in order), **escape, x, info, return**. This places you in a sort of (textual) menu-driven interface to certain software documentation. Menu options are navigated by using the cursor control keys; they are selected by using the return key. Most software uses the info database for the users' manual-sized documents. There's no need for you to worry about whether you can actually access the info database right now; when you get to Lesson 8 and get an introduction to emacs, keep the additional functionality of the info database in mind.

Program and OS Specific

Newer UNIX distributions are coming with documentation built into, or available as an option for, their desktop environments. Sun has their

Answerbook database, which is updated regularly to include helpful information as well as commonly asked questions and their answers. SGI includes what is essentially a set of online books marked up in HTML format. The files include everything from simple help documents to complete editions of several published professional references. Whatever the UNIX you're using, check around for local documentation installed on your machine—it frequently contains large amounts of information compiled in a more convenient form than you'll find anywhere else. Linux, a variation of UNIX, has a large grassroots user base. As a result, most Linux distributions include a great deal of documentation that has been developed and maintained by users. Following is a look at a few of these resources.

THE LINUX HOME PAGE

Even if you're using a commercial UNIX, there are things to be learned from Linux, the publicly-written and supported UNIX variant. As a resource created by users for users, this documentation is frequently the most up-to-date documentation on UNIX freeware/shareware.

The Linux Home Page (http://www.linux.org/) is an excellent starting point; it provides links to vendors, applications, events, and other Linux goodies.

THE LINUX DOCUMENTATION PROJECT

The *Linux Documentation Project* (*LDP*) is a continuously updated collection of information related to Linux. The LDP contains FAQs (Frequently Asked Questions), HOWTOs, and other documentation related to the installation and maintenance of Linux-based systems. This is of value to UNIX users because of the similarity of the two systems. To view the most current information, check the online LDP reference located at: http://sunsite.unc.edu/LDP/.

NEWSGROUPS

Newsgroups provide a less structured approach to finding information, but you'll be surprised at the amount of support you can get from complete strangers. Whatever your need, there is a UNIX newsgroup that can provide answers. To get started, take a look at

```
comp.unix.advocacy
comp.unix.questions
comp.unix.misc
```

THE KDE HELP SYSTEM

If you are using KDE for most of your day-to-day work, you'll be glad to know that KDE has its own built-in HTML help system that is extremely well-integrated into the KDE environment.

Tips of All Sorts   If you don't want to use the full-blown help system, KDE's ToolTips might help you. ToolTips are quick little blips of information that are displayed when you pass your cursor over an icon or menu selection. Not all applications support ToolTips, but if you don't know what something does, pass your cursor over it, wait a few seconds, and see if a ToolTip appears.

Each application has its own help menu that is laid out according to the KDE specification, which maintains consistency across all KDE applications.

To access the help viewer from within an application, simply select **Contents** from the **Help** menu. Figure 2.1 shows the help available from within Karm, the KDE personal information manager.

The KDE help viewer is a full-fledged HTML viewer. You can navigate through the help files by clicking on the links, as you do in any Web browser.

Tip Trick up Your Sleeve   Because the KDE help and file browser is really just an HTML browser, you can use the KDE browser to view any of the other UNIX HTML documentation. Type the URL to the file you want to view into the top of the browser window and press enter.

FIGURE 2.1   KDE has an integrated HTML-based help system.

SUMMARY

There are many help resources available for UNIX. Depending on your needs, you can approach your search for information in several different ways. The methods you are now familiar with are

- **UNIX Manual Pages**—Use the man command to display full information about a specific command. The apropos, man -k, man -f, and whatis commands can display summary information and search for a specific type of command.

- **Built-in Help**—Many programs have built-in help that can be displayed with a command line argument, usually --help or -h.

- **Local Documentation**—Every installation of UNIX ends up with a little something from the personality of the system administrator—so every one is a little different. Local documentation can help you find your way around the places where your installation differs from the collective norm.

- **Online Resources**—The Linux Home Page and Documentation Project provide excellent starting points when wading through the mountains of online Linux information. Remember, even though the information is specifically for Linux, most of it applies to other UNIX variations as well. The `comp.unix.*` newsgroups are also extremely useful for hard-to-find answers.

- **KDE Help System**—KDE provides excellent built-in help for most of its applications. Simply select **Contents** from the **Help** menu that is located in each application.

LESSON 3

THE GRAPHICAL USER INTERFACE

In this lesson, you will learn the basics of the X Windows GUI in addition to enough information to get you started on configuring and customizing your environment.

X WINDOWS OVERVIEW

Although most flavors of UNIX can be accessed via a command-line interface from the console, there is also an easier way. On top of the command-line interface, a variety of *graphical-user-interfaces* (*GUIs*) are available. A few of these GUIs are proprietary, but the majority conform to an open-standard interface called the X Window System, or X Windows. Some manufacturers have extended the X Windows standard with proprietary enhancements. Unfortunately, these enhancements can cause parts of the interface to be incompatible with remote display on other varieties of UNIX. Because the general principles are similar, though, you'll find that a familiarity with one GUI translates well to the others.

X WINDOWS BASICS

Unlike the Macintosh and MS-Windows environments, X Windows is a system that provides a set of interface display functions.

X Marks the Spot   X Windows is usually referred to as X#, where # is the major revision number; or, you might come across X#Rn, where # is the major revision number and n is the minor revision. As of this writing, X11R6 is the current version, but it is generally referred to as X11—or, more simply, just X.

X Windows provides facilities for programs to display windows, buttons, and other user-interactive widgets. It is actually implemented as a type of server program running on the computer. Client programs that want to make use of X Windows display functionality make requests to the server, asking it to perform certain display functions. It does not matter to either the client or server application whether they are running on the same machine or are separated by miles of network—the client makes display requests and the server tries to honor them.

An additional difference between personal computer windowing systems and X Windows is that the interface's look and feel is controlled by a separate program rather than by the X Windows server. In the X Windows model, the X server is responsible for handling client display requests such as requests for displaying windows. However, unless a client specifically draws a title bar for itself, X won't give it one. A separate program must be run to create title bars and to actually manage user interactions such as moving windows around, iconizing/minimizing windows, or providing application-dock functionality.

STARTING X WINDOWS

On many UNIX boxes, the system administrator has configured X so that it starts automatically when the machine boots. If your system does not automatically start X, then you need to start it manually after you log in. The two most common ways to do this are the program `xinit` and a shell script called variably `startx`, `x11`, or `xstart`. If you're on a plain-vanilla Solaris box, you might have to use /usr/openwin/bin/openwin. `startx` (and its variants) is usually a shell script that automates some of the calls to `xinit`. This is a good place to start browsing if you're curious about how things are done and what options are available. (Shell scripts are covered in Lesson 14, "Basic Shell Scripting.")

After the X server itself starts, you need to start some X applications. Usually, a default set of these is started by the automatic execution of the file .xinitrc located in your home directory. Some variants of UNIX don't use this file, or they use it in counter-intuitive ways. For example, IRIX uses .xinitrc if it's present; if not, IRIX uses its own proprietary configuration utility. Some variants of Linux use files named ****.m4. Your system administrator can change the default configuration. If you can't find .xinitrc, you might find that your system remembers what windows you have open and where they are positioned between logins "automagically."

The .xinitrc file—if present—contains a series of lines similar to the following:

```
#!/bin/sh
xrdb -load $HOME/.X11defaults
xscreensaver -timeout 10 &
xterm -geometry 80x30+10+10 &
```

If this in fact was your .xinitrc file, when you started X11 the .xinitrc file would:

- **Line 1**—Run itself via the bourne shell, sh.

- **Line 2**—Load the server resource database (discussed later in this lesson) from the file .X11defaults in your home directory.

- **Line 3**—Start the command xscreensaver, assign a 10-minute timeout, and place it in the background.

- **Line 4**—Start an xterm (terminal), which is 80 characters wide by 30 characters high, placing it 10 pixels from the top and left of your screen.

You'll see more examples of command-line options to X programs later in this lesson.

USING X WINDOWS

The look and feel of X Windows is mostly the responsibility of the particular window-manager you've chosen to run. (You can learn more about window managers and some of their options later in this lesson.) You'll find that there are a number of constants between the various managers. Some of these consistent features might be familiar to anyone who has previously used a computer with a mouse. A few, however, are likely to be new even to users familiar with the Macintosh and MS-Windows environments. The significant things to remember are:

- **X is designed for a three-button mouse**—Most X software makes use of the left button for pointing, clicking, and selection. X uses the center button for general functions such as moving or resizing windows, and the right button for application-specific functions such as opening in-application pop-up menus. Of course, any application is capable of modifying these uses, so examination of the documentation is always appropriate.

- **X has the concept of** *focused input*—On the Macintosh or MS-Windows platforms, if you type on the keyboard you generally expect the typing to appear in whatever window or dialog box is active—this isn't the case with X Windows. In X, the window manager has the option of focusing your input anywhere it chooses. Most window managers can be configured to either focus input on the foremost window, focus input on a selected window (X does not have to be the foremost window), or focus input on whichever window the cursor is over. The last option, although unlike the interface you might be familiar with, is usually considered to be the most powerful. With the window manager configured so that focus follows the cursor, you can direct typing into a mostly hidden window—for example, to start a non-interactive program—by simply moving the cursor over any visible part of the mostly-hidden window and typing. No need to waste time bringing that window to the front, typing the command, and then shuffling the window back underneath the window that you really wanted to be working in.

If Your Input Disappears   If you're typing and you notice that what you're typing isn't appearing where you think it is supposed be, chances are you've got your input focused in some other window. Check to make certain that your cursor is where it belongs, or—if your system is configured for click to focus—that you've clicked where you intend to type. It's very easy to get confused when moving between platforms using different input-focus methods.

In X, the window manager or any other program can attach arbitrary commands to arbitrary user actions. For example, a program can attach the action of displaying a menu when a user right-clicks on the title bar. The window manager can pop-up a variety of menus when the user left-, right-, or center-clicks in the empty background of the windowing system; or it could happen when the user shift-left-, shift-right-, or shift-center-clicks—the possibilities are endless. One popular terminal program, xterm, pops up its configuration menus when the user holds down the control key and left-, right-, or center-clicks in the window. Some window managers attach a standard menu with common commands such as close and resize to each application's title bar. Others attach these functions to pop-up menus or buttons in the title bar. You'll find variations in program behavior even among different installations of the same UNIX flavor. Local configuration options can exert a significant influence over the interface. The best advice on how to find any particular option or command is to read the available documentation and to ask other local users.

Most window managers can iconize windows. Because the actual display of the client program's windows isn't handled by the client, the X server and window manager are free to make some useful contributions to the user experience. One of these contributions is that when the client requests a window with particular characteristics, the server isn't obliged to represent the window that way to the user—it is required only to treat it as though it had those characteristics. This enables the server to, for example, scale the window arbitrarily, or to shrink it down and treat it as an icon. If you're familiar with the idea of a task bar or application dock, you can think of iconized windows as windows that have been minimized, but that you can store anywhere on your screen.

CONFIGURING X WINDOWS

Most configuration of X Windows is handled by a server resource database. When a client makes a request of the server, the server checks this database to determine user preferences for that client. The server resource database is loaded on a per-user basis via the command xrdb, which needs to be executed automatically after starting X11. xrdb loads configuration information from a *dot file* usually named .X11defaults. (Dot files are discussed in Lesson 16, "Modifying the User Environment.") .X11defaults usually contains lines similar to the following:

```
xbiff*onceOnly:                  on
xbiff*wm_option.autoRaise:       off
xbiff*mailBox:                   /usr/spool/mail/mymail
```

If you include these lines in your .X11defaults file, you are telling your X server that if xbiff (an X11 program that notifies you when you have new mail) starts, it needs to set certain options:

- **Line 1**—Sets an xbiff-specific option regarding the frequency of ringing the bell to notify you.

- **Line 2**—Sets an option regarding the window manager's treatment of xbiff—it specifically tells the window manager not to bring xbiff to the front if it's behind other windows when it needs to notify you. (Remember, X11 provides the display and a separate program provides management of things such as window controls.)

- **Line 3**—Tells xbiff where to find the mailbox that it's supposed to look at.

Because each client supports different options and allows the window manager different levels of control, you'll need to consult each client's documentation to learn what you can configure and what you need to do to configure it.

In addition to the server resources database, clients frequently have command-line options that can control the client's interaction with X11. Take a look at the following command:

```
> xterm -fg "black" -bg "white" -fn 6x10 -geometry 85x30+525+1
```

This starts an xterm session with the following configuration: black as the foreground color, white as the background color (black text on a white window), and a 6×10 point font. It also sets the geometry information such that the window is 85 characters wide, 30 characters high, and placed 525 pixels from the left edge of the screen and 1 pixel down from the top.

Again, different programs have different options available and your local documentation is your best source for up-to-date information on your exact configuration.

WINDOW MANAGERS

Because X Windows provides only rudimentary user-interface-component display functionality, an additional program is required to provide a useful user interface. This program is the window manager. Depending on the variation of UNIX you are running, you might have a number of options for different window managers. Each provides slightly different features with accordingly different strengths and weaknesses.

twm

One of the most common—and least-featured—window managers is twm. twm, shown managing the display in Figure 3.1, provides very basic window management functions and is present or available on almost all UNIX implementations. If you work in a multi-platform environment with different flavors of UNIX, you might find twm to be convenient because your configuration can be identical on all the machines. For its simplicity, twm also provides some of the best user extensibility of the interface. If you like, you can create your own standard buttons that appear in your twm title bars to execute arbitrary commands. You can also build your own pop-up menus, automatically execute commands when the cursor enters windows, customize window manager colors and actions by application name and type, and a host of other customizations. To start the twm window manager, execute **twm** after starting X (you can probably do this automatically in your .xinitrc file). The control file for all this customization is named .twmrc and is probably located in your home directory.

As you can see in Figure 3.1, twm enables you to have a number of windows open at once. During window layering—even though windows might be partially covered by one another—you can focus input to the hidden windows, enabling you to work in any open window. Active applications that have been iconized can be clicked to be returned to their normal size.

Iconized Active Applications   twm Title Bar

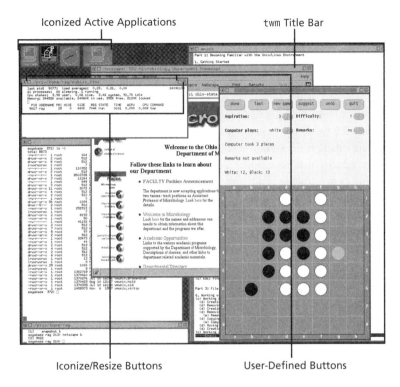

Iconize/Resize Buttons   User-Defined Buttons

FIGURE 3.1   *twm* managing an X Windows session.

OTHER WINDOW MANAGERS

Other window managers you might encounter depending on the variation
of UNIX you are running include

- **olwm**—Sun's default manager for the OpenWindows
  environment.

- **mwm**—The Motif window manager. Many commercial window
  managers are based on, or try to emulate, mwm.

- **4dwm**—The default window manager for SGIs running IRIX.

- **tvtwm**—An experimental extension of twm which includes the
  capability to set up virtual screens.

There are many other window managers, and a variety will most likely be available to you for use on your machine. After you've investigated your options, you can start building a custom environment that feels and behaves exactly as you want it to.

Remember, it is the window manager that provides user-interface features such as title bars. If you find yourself facing a screen which looks like Figure 3.2 (windows missing title bars, no scroll bars, no icons) it is because there is no window manager running; it either hasn't started for some reason, or it has crashed. You can try starting a window manager by typing **twm**—if there is a terminal window open that is accepting keyboard input (directing keyboard input to a particular window is also a window manager function). If not, you'll need to exit the X Windows environment and modify your startup files to start the window manager of your choice immediately after starting the X server.

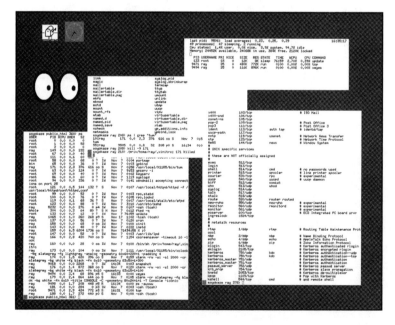

Figure 3.2   This X Windows session has lost its window manager.

DESKTOP ENVIRONMENTS

Historically, window managers have only been used to manage the user's screen. A new type of windowing application is emerging, however. This type functions not only as a window manager in the classical sense, but also provides additional functionality to the user. These desktop environments typically provide sophisticated window management as well as a sort of desktop that is reminiscent of the MS-Windows or Macintosh interface. The desktop frequently includes file management functionality, the capability to create and use icons to launch applications, and an integrated suite of graphical tools for the management and configuration of the computer.

As UNIX vendors try to make their machines more convenient to use, you can expect these desktop environments to become more sophisticated; even today, though, the power and simplicity are quickly approaching that of the popular personal computer interfaces.

Although some of the industry heavy-hitters such as Sun and SGI have weighed in with significant offerings such as OpenWindows and the IRIX desktop, one of the most significant contributions is being made by a nonprofit Internet collaborative effort that is developing the freeware product KDE. KDE is a freely-available and downloadable desktop environment that is compatible with a wide range of UNIX implementations.

KDE

KDE stands for the *K Desktop Environment*, and—according to the authors—the *K* stands for nothing. KDE, rather than one of the commercial desktop environments, is discussed here because of its surprising level of sophistication and its portability to such a wide range of platforms.

 Compatibility   According to the KDE FAQ, KDE is currently known to support Linux, Solaris, FreeBSD, IRIX, and HP-UX, and is expected to be compilable on almost anything which uses the gnu gcc compiler.

KDE provides a sophisticated window manager with convenient extensions such as multiple virtual screens, user-customizable menus, and a facility to automatically remember programs and their placement on the screen between login sessions.

In addition, KDE provides a desktop environment that supports, among other things, icons for files and directories, an application dock, and a quick launch button bar. As you can see in Figure 3.3, the user interface provided by KDE is significantly more user-friendly than the twm (and other typical window manager) interfaces.

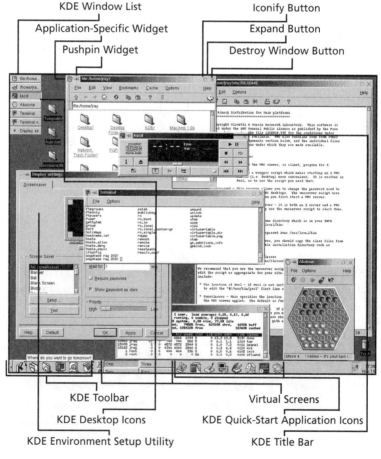

Figure 3.3   KDE makes X Windows friendly.

Following is a look at some of the KDE window features:

- **KDE Window List**—Shows you a list of all the windows that are currently available, even if they're completely hidden on the screen.

- **Application-Specific Widget**—The leftmost widget on the title bar. Its functions are specific to the application associated with the window.

- **Pushpin Widget**—This button locks the window to your display, making it available on any virtual screen you access.

- **Iconify, Expand, and Destroy Window Buttons**—These buttons give you control of the window; minimize it, maximize it, or close it entirely.

- **KDE Quick-Start Application Icons**—Puts you one click away from your most frequently used programs.

- **KDE Toolbar**—This panel includes pop-up menus to start programs, select windows, and configure your environment, as well as other useful utilities.

- **KDE Environment Setup Utility**—Allows you to control such things as your screen saver, display settings, and so on.

- **KDE Desktop Icons**—These icons which live on your desktop represent files, directories, or applications.

In addition to user interface sophistication, KDE provides an integrated suite of tools for configuring your machine and your user interface, and offers a set of useful point-and-click interfaces to general UNIX programs and utilities. Some of these utilities will be discussed in other lessons; so, if you're using a desktop environment of some sort already, pay attention to these sections to see how KDE—and desktop environments in general—can make your life easier.

If you're looking for a way to make your UNIX experience feel a bit more like your personal computer, look into whether your system administrator can install KDE for you.

SUMMARY

This lesson taught you about the background of graphical user interfaces, and about the X Window System in particular. Understanding X Windows will enable you to take advantage of these graphic-based tools.

- X Windows is based on a client/server model. The client runs anywhere you want it to and makes display requests. The server runs on the machine with the display screen and attempts to honor those requests.

- The X Window System requires a window manager to implement user-interface conveniences such as title bars.

- X Windows mice can behave in strange ways—if at first you don't succeed, click and click again.

- X Windows can focus keyboard input to a window in a number of different ways. Pay attention to where your cursor is.

- In the X Windows environment, icons usually represent minimized windows rather than applications.

- The advent of desktop environments is bringing application icons to the world of X Windows.

For all the power of desktop environments, and all the automation of newer window managers, their configurations are usually stored in ugly text files in your home directory. If you want to duplicate your environment from one machine to another, these are a good place to start.

LESSON 4

THE FILE SYSTEM

In this lesson you'll learn the basics of the UNIX file system as well as a few convenient tricks to make your UNIX life easier.

To a beginner, the UNIX file system can appear to be a strange and uninviting place—so many files, and you with just a command line to type at. Bear skin and stone knife time, right? Wrong. Although access to the UNIX file system might initially appear cryptic and primitive, UNIX provides extremely sophisticated file access and control. This sophistication is born of many simple commands from which more complicated commands can be constructed.

FILE SYSTEM DESIGN

Before even the simple commands will make sense, you need to understand a few things about the design of the UNIX file system. Although this might not seem like a very important part of the user experience, the UNIX file system is a bit different than the personal computer file systems you might be familiar with. Actually, you will probably find the biggest differences to be to your liking.

UNIX file systems have a single root directory. Unlike Macintosh file systems with their multiple drive icons on the desktop or Windows file systems with their ABCs, the UNIX file system has a single top-level directory—the *root* directory. UNIX considers its files to be arranged in what is essentially a tree shape, with the root directory as the base, or root. UNIX's tree, however, is upside down as compared to normal trees. The root directory can contain files and other directories, the second-level directories can contain more files and more directories, and so on.

The Powers of Root   UNIX uses the word *root* to describe two different concepts. One is the root user, the person with absolute control over everything having to do with the machine. The other is the root directory, one single specific directory on the machine that is considered to be the top of the file system.

You don't need to care what drives are where. Where do other drives appear, if not named by letters or icons? With UNIX, they appear simply as directories located anywhere in the file system. Odd? Not at all. UNIX completely removes the notion of the hardware and the physical location of the files from the concern of the user. This might take a while to get used to, but when you do you'll see that it makes no sense for a user to have to worry about where a file physically resides. If you know its name and where to find it in the file system, why bother worrying about which chunk of oxidized metal (that's what a hard drive is made of, by the way) it lives upon? If you think about it, you'll see that this has other significant benefits. For example, if your system administrator discovers one day that he's run out of disk space to install new software, he can transparently rearrange disks and files. He can move everything out of some overloaded directory onto a new disk and mount the new disk so that it appears in the same place as the old directory—and you'll never know the difference.

Mounting a drive   The process of telling the file system that the drive exists and at what directory it will appear. On most variations of UNIX, normal users can't mount drives. If you happen to be on a system which enables normal users to mount drives, you need to see your system administrator to find out which drives you can mount, and how to mount them.

As a matter of fact, you don't even need to care what state your files live in. Another benefit of this abstraction is that your system administrator can cause files, directories, or drives which are physically located on distant machines to transparently appear as part of the file system on your machine. The only difference you might notice in accessing remotely-located files might be a slight slowdown due to the network. So, what does this mean? If your system is set up properly, no matter where you are or what machine you sit in front of, whether you're at your main office or halfway around the world, all your files appear in the same place and all your software is where you always expect it to be.

Even if you don't care where your files are, you're always somewhere. UNIX bases most of its notion of the user environment on the user "being somewhere," located and working in some particular directory. With the advent of new graphical desktop environment tools this is becoming less of a universal concept, but is still a good idea to keep in mind when working with UNIX.

UNIX commands and filenames are case sensitive. For both the Windows and Macintosh user, this might come as quite a surprise: UNIX is quite literal in its interpretation of what you type. MyFile doesn't look identical to myfile on paper, and it's not identical to UNIX either. Always note the case of filenames or commands that you are trying to use. Believe it or not, Mail and mail are two different commands, both of which are available on many UNIX variants—and they do two different things!

Files have three attributes. UNIX has a very simple idea of file attributes—files can be readable or not readable, writeable or not writeable, and executable or not executable. Any combination of these options is possible, though some combinations are not particularly sensible. Generally, programs will be readable and executable, and data files will be readable and possibly writeable. UNIX, however, takes you at your word. If you tell it that a data file is executable, for instance, it happily gives you the chance to try to run your Rolodex file—which is unlikely to work; if you tell it that a program is writeable it just as happily enables you to edit your word-processor—which is likely to make the software useless.

Everything belongs to somebody. Every file and directory in the UNIX file system carries around with it information detailing who owns it. The owner of a file can allow or disallow access to a file for other users or other groups of users, and can control whether the file is executable, readable, or writeable.

Now that you understand a bit about what your commands are going to be talking to, you can start learning what you need to know to get around.

NAVIGATING THE FILE SYSTEM

The most basic commands for dealing with the UNIX file system are the ones for moving between directories and finding out what files are in them. Before moving between them though, it's a good idea to know where you are.

WHERE ARE YOU? PWD

The pwd (*present working directory*) command asks your machine to tell you what directory you're currently in. Any time you're running a command line, it's somewhere in the file system—type *pwd* and it tells you where.

For example:

```
> pwd
/priv/home/ray/public_html/
```

Path Particulars   /priv/home/ray/public_html/ is a path. The simplest explanation of a path is the shortest set of directories through which you must travel from the root directory to get to the current file or directory. Each directory in the path is separated by a /.

THE HOME DIRECTORY

To each user, one particular directory is special. This is your *home* directory. From the standpoint of navigating around the file system, this directory is identical to any other; however, it is significant in that when you log on, it is where you will initially be. You can expect that anything in or below your home directory belongs only to you. To make your life easier, UNIX doesn't require you to remember the path to your home directory. Instead, it allows you to refer to your home directory simply as ~, and to anybody else's home directory as *~username*.

Now that you know where you are, the next thing you might want to know is what files are with you.

LISTING FILES

Actually, with UNIX you can list the files just about anywhere, with the exception of places that you don't have permission (more on permissions in Lesson 19, "Permissions"); the easiest place to list files from, though, is "here"—wherever that currently happens to be.

LS

The `ls` command lists files. Issued without arguments, `ls` lists the files and subdirectories in the current directory (the same one `pwd` would tell you about). For example

```
> pwd
/priv/home/ray/public_html/
> ls
cgi_bin                    test.html
images                     vrml
index.html
```

The preceding example shows that your current directory path is /priv/home/ray/public_html and that this directory contains five things. You can't tell from this listing, but cgi_bin, images, and vrml are directories, whereas index.html and test.html are files.

Covering the Bases You didn't really have to issue the `pwd` command to make use of the `ls` command in the preceding example. It's been included for the sake of clarity. If you already know where you are in the file system, there's no reason to ask the computer to repeat it for you.

If you'd like to list the files in some directory other than the current directory, such as the files in the root directory, you can issue the `ls` command with a directory option:

1. Determine the name of the directory you want to list.

2. Issue the *ls* command as: `ls <directory name>`.

If you wanted to list the contents of the root directory /, you would type:

```
> ls /
CDROM                   lib
bin                     priv
core                    tmp
dev                     vmunix
etc                     usr
include                 var
```

Everything here except for vmunix, which is the piece of software at the heart of UNIX, and core, which is an error file that really should be thrown away, are directories.

Filename Facts   Remember that UNIX filenames, and consequently commands, are case-sensitive. UNIX alphabetizes the capitals before the lowercase. This is why CDROM appears before bin.

How can you tell that they are directories? Use option ls to ask it for more information in the listing, specifically the "long" option.

Issue the command as: ls -l <*directory name*>.

```
> ls -l /
total 14
dr-xr-xr-x     2 root          512 Jan  8   1995   CDROM
lrwxrwxr-x     1 root            7 Dec  7   1994   bin ->
/usr/bin
-r－r－r－      1 root      8503728 Oct 25  20:16   core
drwxr-xr-x     3 root        11264 Nov  7  13:02   dev
drwxr-xr-x    11 root         3072 Nov  7  13:01   etc
drwxr-xr-x    46 root         2560 Jan 11   1995   include
drwxr-xr-x    23 root         4096 Oct 13  16:29   lib
drwxr-xr-x     4 root          512 Jul  4   1997   priv
drwxrwxrwx     3 root          512 Nov 24  00:30   tmp
-rwxr-xr-x     1 root      1382769 Aug 12  12:57   vmunix
drwxr-xr-x    29 root         1024 Oct 27  17:53   usr
lrwxrwxr-x     1 root            8 May 21   1995   var ->
↳/usr/var
```

ls Variations   Different versions of UNIX have ls commands which produce slightly different output. No matter what flavor of ls you have, you will see fields similar to these—and maybe a few others. At this time, don't concern yourself with any extra fields that appear.

This listing might look a little convoluted at first, but the parts that you need to understand at this point are fairly straightforward.

- First comes a line telling you how many things are in this directory—in this case, 14.

- Next come lines detailing the contents of the directory, one per item.

- The ten characters that look like random gibberish at the left of each line are actually the attribute information for the file. The first character of this tells you whether the line is for a directory; lines having the first character d are for directories. Lines which start with a - are for normal files. Sharp observers might note that the lines for bin and var start with an l. This indicates that these are actually *links*, or alternative names for other files or directories (links are discussed in greater depth later in this lesson). The remaining nine characters are three sets of three that indicate, respectively, the read, write, and execute status of the file for the file's owner, the file's group, and everybody else. You'll learn about how to manipulate these settings, as well as more about the idea of file ownership, groups, and "everybody else," in Lesson 19.

- Shortly after the ten characters of permission information, each line contains root. This is the owner of the file or directory. In the case of the preceding example, the root user owns everything in the directory. If you see a double column of entries containing root, it's because your ls command displays group information as well as user information. Don't concern yourself with the second of these columns until you become familiar with groups in Lesson 19.

- Next comes a number, sometimes small and sometimes large. This is the amount of disk space that the file or directory occupies. For directories it's not the space that the contents of the directory occupy, but rather the space occupied by the data file which controls the directory. This value is in bytes. As you can see, the directories take up very little room—although their contents might be a different story. Conversely, vmunix takes roughly 1.4Mb, and that pesky core file which should have been deleted ages ago is taking up 8.5Mb.

- After the file size comes the date of the most recent modification of the file. If the file was modified within the last year, the date and time are given; otherwise, a date and year are given.

- Finally comes the filename. Note that the filenames are identical to the names given by the version of ls from the previous example, with the exception of bin and var, which have a funny *pointer* that points to a path. As previously mentioned, these are actually alternative names for other directories, and the pointer is pointing at the path to which they are linked.

You have by now perhaps noticed that the total line claims that this directory contains 14 items, but that only 12 appear in the listing. This is because UNIX, as a courtesy, hides some files from the user unless they are specifically asked for. Files whose names begin with a . (dot) are not shown by default. Typically, control and configuration files—which you do not want to see cluttering up your directory listing—are named with a dot so that you don't have to see them in everyday use. Nevertheless, if you want to see them, all you have to do is ask. In this case, use the **all** option for **ls**.

```
>ls -al /
total 14
drwxr-xr-x    1 root           8 Nov 24  00:30  .
-rwx - - -    1 root          42 Dec 13  1997   .login
dr-xr-xr-x    2 root         512 Jan  8  1995   CDROM
lrwxrwxr-x    1 root           7 Dec  7  1994   bin ->
/usr/bin
-r - r - r -  1 root     8503728 Oct 25  20:16  core
drwxr-xr-x    3 root       11264 Nov  7  13:02  dev
drwxr-xr-x   11 root        3072 Nov  7  13:01  etc
drwxr-xr-x   46 root        2560 Jan 11  1995   include
```

```
drwxr-xr-x   23 root         4096 Oct 13  16:29  lib
drwxr-xr-x    4 root          512 Jul  4   1997  priv
drwxrwxrwx    3 root          512 Nov 24  00:30  tmp
-rwxr-xr-x    1 root       1382769 Aug 12  12:57  vmunix
drwxr-xr-x   29 root         1024 Oct 27  17:53  usr
lrwxrwxr-x    1 root            8 May 21   1995  var ->
➥/usr/var
```

Note that two new lines have appeared in the listing: a line for a file cryptically named . and a line for a file named .login. The .login file is a typical UNIX configuration file; expect to see files of this nature in any directory used as a home directory. The . file might be a little less expected; however, it is quite normal. The directory . exists in every directory on a UNIX machine and is essentially synonymous with the current directory. For example, the command ls, and the command ls . produce identical results because ls defaults to listing the current directory and . is the current directory.

The root directory / is unique in that it does not have a directory named .. in it. The directory .. means "the directory preceding this one." Therefore, if you're currently in /priv/home/ray/public_html, ls .. produces a listing of /priv/home/ray.

The ls command has many options in addition to the ones discussed here: options for sorting, options for tabulating the data, and options for adding flags to the "short" listing to show the file's attributes. Beyond the -l and -a options discussed previously, the next most useful are the -F option, which indicates file attributes, and the -R option, which recursively lists all files below the specified directory.

CHANGING DIRECTORIES: cd

Now that you know how to find out where you are and what's around you, it's time to wander around a bit. To move from one directory to another, use the UNIX command cd. If you want to move from wherever you currently are to another directory, you

1. Determine where your current location (use the pwd command if you don't already know).

2. Pick a directory to which you'd like to go (/usr/local for this example).

3. Issue the cd command as: cd <directory name>

For example:

```
> pwd
/priv/home/ray/public_html
> cd /usr/local
> pwd
/usr/local
```

The final pwd shows /usr/local as the current directory, which is exactly what was wanted.

pushd AND popd

An even more powerful way of changing between directories is to make use of the directory stack.

 Stack   In computer-speak, a *stack* is a type of data storage which works for data much like a stack of dishes. With the dish-stack, dishes can only be added to the pile or taken off of the pile from the top, and the most recently added plate is the first to be removed. Data storage stacks work in exactly the same way. Data is pushed onto the stack, burying previous data, and popped off of the stack, uncovering previous data.

If you are currently in one directory and want to change temporarily to another, there is an easier way to do it than with two cd commands. By making use of the pushd command, you can place the current directory on the directory stack and change your current directory to the new directory. When you are ready to return to your previous directory, simply use popd to get your old directory back.

If you want to change from your current directory to another, and then return automatically, make use of the pushd and popd commands as follows:

1. Decide where you want to go.

2. Issue the pushd command as: **pushd <*directoryname*>**.

3. You are now in your new directory and can work here for as long as you like. Your previous directory is waiting for you on the stack.

4. When you are finished and want to return to your previous directory, issue the popd command as: **popd.**

For example:

```
> pwd
/usr/local
> pushd /var/adm
/var/adm /usr/local
> pwd
/var/adm
```

...now you can work here as long as you like.

```
> popd
/usr/local
> pwd
/usr/local
```

If you'd like to try this out on your system, and you've tried using the ls command to list your root directory, you have a variety of directories to try. If the directory /usr is present (and it almost universally is), you can try the pushd and popd command out by using **pushd /usr**, browsing around, and then using **popd** to come back to wherever you are now.

You now know almost everything about navigating around the UNIX file system, but before going on to other topics there's one additional variation that you need to be aware of.

RELATIVE AND ABSOLUTE PATHS

Up to this point, all paths you have been working with have been *absolute paths*—that is, paths starting with the root directory and ending in a file or directory name. In real life you would quickly find this annoying, so UNIX provides the concept of a *relative path* as well. Relative paths are relative to the current directory. With the addition of relative paths to your toolkit, if the current directory is /usr/local/ and you want to be in the directory /usr/local/bin/, you have the option of issuing two different cd commands. You can type either **cd /usr/local/bin** or **cd bin**; either results in your new current directory being /usr/local/bin. You can also use the directory element .., discussed previously as a relative path component. If, for example, you are in /usr/local/bin and want to be in /usr/local/lib, you have a choice of `cd /usr/local/lib`, or `cd ../lib`.

 Path Do's and Don'ts   All absolute paths start with /; all relative paths do not.

By this point you know how to find out where you are, what files are in what directories, and how to move around to different directories. Now it's time to learn a few tricks.

FILENAME EXPANSION IN SUPPORTED SHELLS

Some shells (tcsh and bash being the most prevalent of these) support filename expansion. Essentially, this is a way of getting the shell to do some of your typing for you. If your shell supports filename expansion, you can use this feature by hitting the **Tab** key after typing the beginning—hopefully enough of the beginning to uniquely identify the file—of the filename or directory name. For example, if you want to edit a pre-existing file named mybigfile.dat which is located in your current directory, you might issue the command: `vi mybi<tab>`. (vi is an editor which will be discussed in Lesson 8, "Text Editing.") If you have no other files that start with the characters "mybi" in the current directory, the shell automatically completes the filename for you. If you do have other files which start with "mybi," the shell beeps at you and you have to type more of the filename to make it unique before trying the **Tab** key again.

Remember, all these techniques can be used together. If you're working in /usr/local/bin, and suddenly remember that you forgot to edit some files in /usr/local/myincludes, you can get there with *pushd ../myin<tab>*, and back again with *popd*.

NAVIGATING THE FILE SYSTEM USING KDE

If you find moving around the command line to be awkward, you'll be happy to know that KDE provides a very user-friendly way to navigate the file system. Beating Windows 98 to the idea of a Web-based desktop, KDE's file management system is also based on the philosophy that "Everything is a Web page." Each file manager window supports the full functionality of a normal Windows or MacOS window but is also a full-fledged Web browser. Breaking slightly from the double-click model that you're undoubtedly used to, KDE only requires a single-click to perform its actions.

SIMPLE KDE ACTIONS

In KDE, files are represented with icons that usually indicate the file type. Directories are shown as folders. Double clicking a directory is similar to using **cd** to get to that directory from the command line; a new window will open up to display the contents of that directory. Figure 4.1 shows a KDE file manager window.

 Navigating Your Files Notice that the file manager window displays the URL of the directory it is showing. Because each window is a Web browser, you can substitute a Web or FTP address into the URL field and KDE immediately takes you there—assuming you have an Internet connection, of course!

As you'd expect, to move or copy files between locations you can simply drag files from one location to another. A pop-up menu appears at the end of the drag, asking if you'd like to copy or move the files. This is an example of a *contextual menu*, which appears when an action is performed within a certain context.

To delete files, drag the files you want to erase to the **Trash** icon. Click on the icon with your right mouse button and choose **Empty Trash Bin** to complete the action.

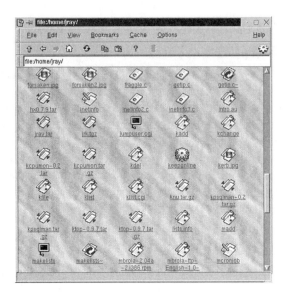

FIGURE 4.1 KDE looks and acts similar to other popular desktop environments.

Use the following steps to create a new folder:

1. Right-click in the location where you want the folder to appear.

2. Choose **New** from the pop-up contextual menu.

3. Select **Folder** from its submenu.

Getting Home If you need to get to your home directory in KDE, just look for the icon of a folder with a little house on it. Clicking on this icon opens a KDE file manager window showing your home directory.

If you spend a few minutes playing around with KDE, you'll find that its simplicity and elegance are on-par with commercial desktop operating systems. If you've previously worked with personal computers, you might find it a bit difficult to believe that in the world of UNIX, most of the truly great software is user written, community supported, based on open standards, and completely free! It scares the bejeezus out of the big OS manufacturers.

There's quite a bit to explore, so if you're running a KDE system, take a few minutes to look around before you continue on to Lesson 5, "Finding Files."

SUMMARY

This lesson has given you the basic skills to work within the file system and a typical environment. If you have any problems with this material, please practice it before moving to the next lesson. Following is a review of some of this lesson's specifics:

- UNIX abstracts the physical location of the data. Don't worry about where your data and software physically reside—if your system administrator is doing his or her job, it doesn't matter.

- UNIX is case-sensitive. Pay careful attention to case, especially if you're transferring files between a UNIX machine and a personal computer.

- UNIX files have attributes of readability, writeability, and executeability. You can set the attributes of a file that you own such that you cannot execute it, cannot write it, and cannot read it. You do not want to do this.

- The pwd command tells you where you are.

- The ls command tells you what files are in a directory.

- The cd command takes you places.

- The pushd command remembers where you were and the popd command takes you back again.

- Use relative paths when you can. If the directory is near your current directory, it's usually much more convenient to use a relative path from you current directory than to use the absolute path from /.

- Remember that all these features and commands work together.
  UNIX is about combining many small programs and features
  that do small parts of the job you need done into a convenient
  tool which performs precisely as you want it to.

- Desktop environments can make your life easier— they automate some of the routine day-to-day tasks and provide a friendly
  face for some of the more difficult ones. If your system doesn't
  have KDE, don't fret—chances are that either KDE can be
  installed on it (if you're nice enough to your system administrator), or it already comes with a nice desktop environment with
  comparable capabilities.

Lesson 5

Finding Files

In this lesson you will learn to use some of UNIX's built-in search tools to find files.

In Lesson 4, "The File System," you learned how to list the files in directories and to navigate from one directory to another. You probably also noticed that there are a lot of files included in a standard UNIX distribution. You're certain to run into the situation where you know the name of a file you want to use, but have no idea where it's located. Rather than using **cd** and **ls** to find your way through the entire file system, you can use some of UNIX's search utilities to help locate what you need.

Finding Files

In order to locate a file, you need to know something about it: a portion of its name, when it was created, or perhaps its size. Armed with these pieces of information, you can dispatch the `find` command and allow it to scour the file system looking for matches to your query.

Finding a File by Name

The most common type of search is by filename. You've probably used a `find file` command on other operating systems that works similarly. You supply the filename, or portion of the filename, to be found, and the system returns a list of matches.

 Using find Before you try out the `find` command, there's something you need to know. If you run `find` on a large file system, especially one mounted over the network, it's likely to take a very long time.

To search for a file by name, use the following steps:

1. Determine the name of the file you want to search for. If you want to, you can include wildcards in the search for the filename.

2. Choose a starting directory for the search. If you want to search the entire file system, the starting directory will be /.

3. Invoke the find command as find <starting directory> -name <filename> -print.

For example:

```
>find / -name sound -print
/usr/src/linux-2.0.34/drivers/sound
/usr/src/linux-2.0.35/drivers/sound
/var/lock/subsys/sound
/etc/rc.d/init.d/sound
```

Search Errors   If you're searching the entire file system, you're likely to encounter errors such as

```
find: /home/ftp/bin: Permission denied
find: /home/ftp/etc: Permission denied
```

This is entirely normal, and isn't cause for alarm. The system is simply telling you that in scanning through the file system searching for files, it has hit directories that you don't have permission to read. If you confine the search to your home directory (which can be represented to the system as ~/), you don't see any of these errors.

The system has responded to the request by finding four different files named sound. Because find was instructed to search the entire file system, the search took more than a minute; there are hundreds of directories and thousands of filenames that were just processed.

You might wonder why you need to follow the command by -print. This is necessary because find is capable of doing things other than simply

telling you about what it has found. On the other hand, if you don't issue
the -print option, most versions of find will happily go out, find the files
for you, and quit—all without telling you a thing. Remember, UNIX takes
what you tell it very literally.

FINDING A FILE BY DATE

Imagine you just created a document file on the system but you can't
remember its name. How in the world can you find it? One possible solution is to search by time, finding files that are younger than a certain time.
To search for a file by its creation date do the following:

1. Determine the relative age of your file in days.

2. Choose a starting directory for the search. Remember, / searches
   the entire file system, whereas ~/ searches only your personal
   directory.

3. Invoke find using the -ctime option: **find** *<starting
   directory>* **-ctime** *<days old>* **-print**.

For example:

```
>find ~/ -ctime 2 -print
/home/jray/getip.c
/home/jray/a.out
/home/jray/getip2.c
/home/jray/.saves-8395-postoffice
```

If you entered this command, you'd have searched your home directory
for files that have been modified in the last two days (48 hours). If these
were your results, one of these four files would be the one that you were
trying to find.

FIND A FILE BY SIZE

The advantage of finding a file by size might not be immediately obvious
until your system begins to run out of room. UNIX will often save a file
called core when a program crashes; this is referred to as a *core dump*.
The core file contains all the information that was in memory when the
program crashed, and can be used by the programmers to debug what
went wrong. Usually the core file can be erased unless you'd like to try

debugging the program yourself. The problem with these files is that they tend to get written in directories that you might not be aware of, and silently consume drive space without your knowledge. Of course, if you're out of disk space, you're interested in finding large files that might have been created by other processes as well; so, just finding core by name will not do. To search by size use the following steps:

1. Choose a target file size for which you'd like to search, and find will locate all files of this size (or larger) for you.

2. Choose a starting directory.

3. Start the find program using the -size option: **find <starting directory> -size <k> -print.**

For example:

```
>find ~/ -size 1024k -print
/home/jray/bochs/bochs-980513/core
/home/jray/postgres51/core
```

The find command you see here has located two core files (which hopefully won't actually be in your home directory) that are 1024k or more in size. If there had been other large files, they would have been listed as well; in this case, though, only core files were found.

There are many other command line switches that can by used with find besides -name, -ctime, and -size. Be sure to check out the find man pages if you're interested in learning more.

whereis

The whereis command performs a quick search on a preset number of directories, and returns paths to source code, binaries, and man pages for the file you specify. It is less useful as a general find utility than find but might still come in handy.

For example:

```
>whereis time
time: /usr/bin/time /usr/include/time.h /usr/man/man2/time.2
➡/usr/man/mann/time.n
```

The whereis command shows that the time binary is located in /usr/bin/time, whereas the header file is in /usr/include/time.h. Two man page paths are also returned. If you're interested in finding where programs and their associated files are located on your machine, whereis might do the trick.

which

Lastly, the which command can also help you locate files that are contained within one of the directories specified in your PATH environment variable. Lesson 16, "Modifying the User Environment," discusses how you can go about configuring the PATH variable. This is less useful as a method of finding files than as a way to find out which version of a program executes when you type a command. For example, if your system has two different programs named *time*, you can use the which command to find out which one runs when you type time. You can invoke which much like you did whereis—just supply a filename for it to look up.

For example:

```
>which time
/usr/bin/time
```

UNIX returns the full path to the time command. The which command is the least configurable of the commands you've seen so far, but it is also the fastest. If you're ever trying to remember where a program is located, give which a shot.

FINDING FILES THAT CONTAIN A WORD OR PATTERN

One of the most powerful built-in programs in UNIX is grep. The grep utility enables you to quickly search through the body of files for a particular word or pattern. grep comes in three flavors: grep, egrep, and fgrep. The differences between these versions are based on the complexity of the *regular expressions* that they can handle. Regular expressions define a pattern of text that can be used to search files when a specific word or phrase to be searched for might not be known. (You will learn more about regular expressions in Lesson 13, "Regular

Expressions.") The `fgrep` command is the fastest of the three, but handles the least complex expressions. To be safe, you can always use plain `grep`, which will work the same in every case, on every system. So, how do you use this wonderful tool? Simple—just give it the word or pattern to look for, and the files you want searched:

1. Choose the word or phrase you want to find.

2. Find the filename you want to search. If it is in another directory, you must specify the entire pathname. You can also use wildcards to search multiple files.

3. Type `grep` *`<pattern to find> <file or files to search>`* at the command prompt.

For example:

```
>grep "jray" *.txt
8979-10.txt:<manager>=jray
log.txt: Access by jray on 11/12/98
kiwi.txt: jray loves to eat kiwis.  But don't you think that
➥it would be
```

This example searches for `jray` in any file that ends in .txt. It has turned up three files—8979-10.txt, log.txt, and kiwi.txt—that contain the string; each filename is followed by the text that contains `jray`. Two options you might want to consider adding to `grep` are `-i` to ignore case and `k -n` to display the line numbers of the match in each file. You can add these flags to the command line, immediately following the `grep` command.

The `grep` command is an extremely valuable tool that will become even more valuable later when you learn about regular expressions. Remember to turn back to this lesson to test some of the things you'll learn in Lesson 13.

USING THE KDE FIND FEATURE

For those of you who are running KDE, you'll be glad to know that KDE has a built-in find utility that offers many of the same features of the command-line versions of `find` and `grep`. KDE has provided a friendly face to these functions that will seem quite familiar to anyone who has run a search under MacOS or Windows computers. The KDE Find Utility is shown in Figure 5.1.

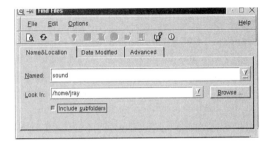

Figure 5.1   KDE provides a friendly interface to the UNIX *find* and *grep* utilities.

To search in the KDE environment, use the following steps:

1. Click the **K** toolbar icon to bring up the main KDE menu.

2. Choose **Find Files**.

3. Select the appropriate search criteria from one of the three tabs.

4. Click the small magnifying glass in the **Find Files** toolbar to locate the matching files.

There are three different tabs in **Find Files** that conduct three different sorts of searches:

- **Name & Location**—If you're searching for a filename, this is the tab you need to use. You can type in a partial filename and supply a starting directory for the search. This is equivalent to the find -name command you used earlier.

- **Date Modified**—Like the find -ctime option already discussed, the **Date Modified** tab enables you to search your file system based on file modification dates.

- **Advanced**—The advanced options enable you to locate files of a specific type or search the contents of files for a word or phrase.

Of course you can continue to use the command line utilities from within KDE, but if you're more comfortable with pointing and clicking, it's nice to know you have the option to do so.

SUMMARY

Finding something on a UNIX-based computer can be a bit difficult with the huge number of files and directories that are available to be searched. Thankfully, UNIX provides a set of powerful utilities to help you find what you are looking for. In this lesson, you have learned several techniques for locating files based on their names and attributes. You are also now familiar with searching the contents of files for a particular word or phrase.

- **find**—The find command can search the entire UNIX file system, or the area under any directory, for a particular file based on a variety of criteria. You have seen how to use it to find files based on name, creation date, and size.

- **whereis**—If you're looking for a program file, its source, or its man pages, the whereis command might work for you. whereis searches a preset list of common file locations and quickly returns paths to anything it finds.

- **which**—The which function is dependent on your PATH environment variable. It searches the paths that you have specified for a particular file name.

- **grep (grep/egrep/fgrep)**—The grep command set is an extremely powerful method of searching the actual content of files for a particular word or pattern. The power of the grep command, when coupled with regular expressions (see Lesson 13), is incredible.

- **Find Utility**—KDE provides an easy-to-use interface that encompasses many of the features of find and grep.

LESSON 6

WORKING WITH FILES ON THE SHELL

In this lesson, you will learn how to perform basic file maintenance functions such as creating and deleting files and directories.

It is unlikely that you will make use of any UNIX commands more frequently than the file maintenance command set. Thankfully, the commands you'll use the most are very short and have only a few important options. Although these commands and options might initially seem simplistic, between what you can do with them and what you'll learn about automating them in Lesson 14, "Basic Shell Scripting," you'll find that these commands can perform almost any file maintenance task you can imagine.

WORKING WITH FILES AND FOLDERS: THE COMMAND LINE

The command line is your primary interface to the UNIX file system as well as your primary tool for creating, deleting, and rearranging your files. It's not unusual for pieces of software to provide file creation and deletion tools, but these are rarely as powerful as the command line. Even if you intend to avoid the command line for your day-to-day work, you'll want to know about these tools.

Tweedle Dee   When working with the command line, remember this: filenames that you give as arguments to commands can be either relative or absolute paths. This means that if you have a command named `twee-dle`, which twiddles a file, if you type

tweedle myfile, you twiddle the file myfile in the current directory.

tweedle ../myfile, you twiddle the file myfile in the directory directly above this one.

tweedle /priv/home/henry/myfile, you twiddle the file myfile in the directory /priv/home/henry (assuming that you have permission to twiddle files in that directory, of course).

Keep in mind that `tweedle` in the preceding example is a hypothetical command with hypothetical results— UNIX has no such command. It is used here simply to help explain a "modifies in some unspecified way" command. You can substitute any operation you want for `twiddle`/`tweedle`.

CREATING A NEW EMPTY FILE: touch

The `touch` command is used to update the "last modified" time of a file and set it to the current time. This might seem like an odd thing to want to do, but it's a very useful utility if you have an application that performs some function on files newer than a particular time.

Taking Advantage of touch   One place you might want to remember that you can use the touch command is with backup and archiving software. Many whole-system backup programs default to only backing up files which were modified since the last backup (this is called and *incremental* backup). If you want to make sure that a file is backed up, even though you've not modified it recently, you can *touch* the file to change the modification date and make it appear to have been modified at the time you touched it.

A useful side effect of touching a file is that if the file that you try to *touch* doesn't exist, touching it causes it to be created as a new empty file.

If you need to update the modification date of a file or create a new empty file, do the following:

1. Determine the filename or filenames of the file or files you want to either update or create.

2. Issue the touch command as: **touch** **_<filename>_** **_<filename>_** ....

For example, type

> **touch myfile**

If myfile previously existed, its last-modified date would now be set to the current time. If myfile did not previously exist, it would now exist as an empty file with a last-modification date of the current time.

Of course, if you want to create multiple files or update the modification dates on multiple files, you might type something such as

> **touch myfile1 myfile2 myotherfile**

This results in myfile, myfile2, and myotherfile all having updated modification dates or being created as necessary.

Additional Use of touch When you become comfortable enough with UNIX to start automating your work using shell scripting (discussed in Lesson 14), you will find the touch command useful for creating *flag files* that allow your scripts to talk to each other. Keep the touch command in mind when thinking about uses for conditional statements.

REMOVING FILES: rm

Now that you know how to create a file, it's appropriate to learn how to get rid of it. The rm command deletes files.

The Power of rm rm is a very powerful command, and one that you need to be just a bit afraid of. There is not a long-time UNIX user alive who has not mistyped arguments to the rm command and then watched in considerable dismay as a large fraction of their file system evaporated. The rm command can remove as precisely as a scalpel or as indiscriminately as a ton of dynamite. Be careful out there!

Follow these steps to use the rm command to delete files:

1. Determine which file, or files, you want to delete.

2. Issue the rm command as rm *<file1>* *<file2>* *<file3>* ....

You can simultaneously remove as many files as you want to. For example, if you want to delete the files myfile and myotherfile, use the following rm command:

```
> rm myfile myotherfile
```

After issuing the rm command for the files you want to delete, you might be presented with a response such as

```
remove myfile (y/n)?
```

This is the rm interactive mode, a protective measure designed to make certain that you really mean to delete the files that you specified (if you really want to, hit **y**). Usually your system administrator will have configured your system so that rm operates in interactive mode by default. In Lesson 16, "Modifying the User Environment," you will learn how to change this default—but you are advised to leave it in interactive mode until you've decided that you're comfortable with UNIX.

OPTIONS TO rm

The rm command supports several useful options:

- **i**—interactive. i makes rm ask you to confirm the deletion of each file before it is actually deleted. As annoying as this might seem, if your system administrator hasn't configured your account to use rm in interactive mode by default, get used to issuing the rm command as **rm -i <file1> <file2>....**

- **f**—force. f requests that rm carry out deletions regardless of the file permissions. Remember, you can create files and set the permissions so that even you, as the owner, can't read or write the file. If you don't use force mode, rm asks you if you want to override the permissions whenever it tries to delete files that you can't write.

- **r**—recursive. r is a very powerful option to rm; the recursive mode is not for the faint of heart. When you issue the rm command as **rm -f <directoryname>**, rm recursively deletes the directory and all its contents. If the directory contains other directories, they are deleted in the same manner.

CREATING A DIRECTORY: mkdir

Directories are very useful for organizing files into sensible groupings. Use the following steps if you need to create a directory:

1. Decide what you want to call the directory.

2. Issue the mkdir command as **mkdir <directoryname>**.

For example

```
> mkdir fresh_new_direcotry
```

This creates a new directory named fresh_new_direcotry, which will be located in the current directory. Unfortunately, *directory* is misspelled, so you'll need the next command as well. As with touch, you might want to use mkdir to create a few extra directories so that you can remove them with the next command, rmdir.

REMOVING AN EMPTY DIRECTORY: rmdir

It isn't very helpful for organization to have old directories that you no longer need laying around, so occasionally you might need to delete one. The command rmdir deletes empty directories. Follow these steps to use rmdir to delete a directory:

1. Decide which directory or directories you want out of your way.

2. Issue the rmdir command as **rmdir <directory1> <directory2> <directory3>....**

For example

```
> rmdir fresh_new_direcotry an_old_directory/kludge
```

This deletes the misspelled directory from the previous example; it also deletes the directory named kludgedir that is located in the directory an_old_directory in this example.

The rmdir command does not affect directories that aren't empty, so it's a convenient command to use to clean house if you've got a bunch of directories laying around. You can get it to try to delete everything in the current directory by issuing the following command:

```
> rmdir *
```

You're not expected to understand this syntax yet—you'll get to that in Lesson 13, "Regular Expressions." Furthermore, you're likely to get dozens of error messages in response to typing this command; but the end result of issuing rmdir in this fashion is that any empty directories in this directory go away, and nothing else is affected.

REMOVING FILES AND DIRECTORIES AT THE SAME TIME: rm -r

Because the `rmdir` command only works on empty directories, you'll eventually want a way to delete a directory as well as all its contents. For this, the `rm` command in recursive mode is the solution. Follow these steps if you need to delete a directory and all its contents:

1. Determine the name of the directory that you want to delete.

2. Issue the `rm` command as **rm -r *<directoryname>*.**

For example, type

```
> rm -r /priv/home/henry/junkdirectory
```

This removes the directory /priv/home/henry/junkdirectory and recursively removes all its contents.

If you manage to delete your current directory (not a fun thing to do), you'll eventually end up getting error messages saying `Cannot stat current directory`, `can't stat .` and `. not found`. How long it takes UNIX to figure out that you're suddenly located "nowhere" depends on which commands you run, but you can always rescue the situation by typing **cd ~/** to get back to your home directory.

COPYING FILES: cp

If you need to make copies of files, you need the `cp` command. This command can either copy a single file to a new destination file, or copy one or more files to a single destination directory.

Follow these steps to use the `cp` command to make a copy of a single file:

1. Determine the source filename, and the destination filename to which you'd like to copy it.

2. Issue the `cp` command as **cp *<sourcefile>* *<destinationfile>*.**

To use the cp command to copy one (or more) files to a destination directory, follow these steps:

1. Determine all the source filenames and the name of the destination directory. The cp command will not create the destination directory for you, so if it doesn't exist you'll need to use the mkdir command first.

2. Issue the cp command as **cp <source1> <source2> ... <destinationdir>**.

For example, type the command

```
> cp myfile1 /priv/home/henry/myfile2
```

The example shown here copies the file myfile1 from the current directory and places the copy in /priv/home/henry/myfile2.

Following is its second form:

```
> cp /etc/sendmail.cf /priv/home/henry/myfile2 myfile1 /tmp
```

This time it would copy the file sendmail.cf from the directory /etc, the file myfile2 from the directory /priv/home/henry, and myfile1 from the current directory, and then place the copies in the directory /tmp.

Remember that you don't have to copy multiple files to use the "into a directory" version—just give it the one filename and the destination directory.

COPYING DIRECTORIES: cp -r

Just like the rm command has a recursive mode for removing directories, the cp command has a recursive mode for copying directories. If you issue the cp command with the -r option, it attempts to treat each of the source filenames as directories and recursively copies them to the destination directory. Follow these steps to use the cp command in this way:

1. Determine the names of the directories that you'd like to copy.

2. Issue the cp command as **cp -r <source1> <source2> ... <destdir>**.

For example, issue the command

```
> cp -r /usr/local/httpd/logs /tmp
```

The cp command creates a new directory named logs in the directory /tmp, and makes a copy of the contents of the directory /usr/local/httpd/logs in this new /tmp/logs directory.

MOVING FILES AND DIRECTORIES: mv

If you simply need to move (rename) files rather than copying them, you want to use the mv command. This command uses the same two forms that the cp command does: The first moves (renames) a file from one name to another name, and the second moves one or more files to a destination directory.

Follow these steps to use the mv command to rename a single file:

1. Determine the current name of the file and the name you'd prefer it to have.

2. Issue the mv command as: mv *<currentname>* *<newname>*.

For example, if you have a file named todays_mail and want to store it away with your backed up email, you might type

```
> mv todays_mail ~/mymaildir/June10.mail
```

This command would move the file todays_mail in the current directory to the file June10.mail located in the directory ~/mymaildir (remember, that's the directory mymaildir located in your home directory).

Follow these steps to use the mv command to move one or more files to a new location:

1. Determine the names of all the files you want to move and the name of the directory to which you'd like to move them.

2. Issue the mv command as mv *<file1>* *<file2>* ... *<destinationdir>*.

For example

```
> mv /usr/local/httpd/logs/error_log /priv/home/henry/myfile2
➡/tmp
```

This command moves the file error_log from the directory /usr/local/httpd/logs, and the file myfile2 from the directory /priv/home/henry into the directory /tmp.

Limitations to mv   The mv command can also be used to move and rename directories with exactly the same syntax used for moving and renaming files—just give directory names instead of filenames.

Unfortunately, for this task the mv command is a little more limited than you might like it to be. It cannot move directories between physical devices; so every now and then if you try to move a directory from one location to another, UNIX's abstraction of physical devices in the file system will sneak up to bite you, and you get an error message such as:

```
Can't move directories across partitions
```

If this happens, the easiest solution is to use the copy command to copy the offending directory, and then delete the original.

CREATING LINKS: ln

The final file management utility you will learn about in this lesson is the command used for creating links or aliases to files. The ln command is used to create links to files so that one file can appear to be in multiple locations and have multiple names.

To see the utility of this command, consider the situation in which you want your friends to look at your daily schedule. Daily or weekly, as appropriate, you can create a new file with your schedule and name it with the current date. Because you don't want to have to constantly give your friends new filenames to check your schedule, you might just create a link named myschedule, which you then point to whatever file contains your current schedule. Your friends can always look at myschedule to get your schedule, and you can keep your daily planner archives neatly arranged.

Follow these steps to use the ln command to create a link:

1. Determine the name of the file to which you want a link. The ln command is willing to create links to non-existent files, which isn't particularly useful, so make certain you know the correct name of the file you want to link.

2. Determine the alternate name by which you want to be able to access the file.

3. Issue the ln command as **ln -s <realfilename> <alternate-name>**. Don't worry about the significance of the -s command. This signifies that the link is a *soft link*, the kind common in everyday use, as opposed to a *hard link* that isn't really useful to non-administrative types.

For example, if you wanted to be able to easily browse your Web server log file, you might issue the command

```
> ln -s /usr/local/httpd/logs/access_log ~/weblog
```

If you were to do this, you would create a link named weblog in your home directory. This link would be an alternative name for the file /usr/local/httpd/logs/access_log.

You can work with this link almost exactly as though it were the real file. If you try to read its contents, you read the contents of the real file. If you try to modify or edit it, you edit the contents of the real file. If you delete the link, however, you only delete the link; the real file remains. So that you can tell the link apart from the real file, if you ls -l the link it shows up as a filename that points to another path.

```
> ls -l ~/weblog
lrwxrwxr-x  1 ray       7 Nov 28   1998  weblog ->
➡/usr/local/httpd/logs/access_log
```

Web Server Tip   One very useful place to use the `ln` command is when working with Web servers—if you're not going to be using a Web server, ignore this tip. Many Web-servers serve a file named index.html by default if the user doesn't specify a filename in their URL. If you want a page to display by default, and don't want to have to name it index.html, you can just make a link to the real file named index.html and the server will never know the difference.

SUMMARY

In this lesson you learned a set of commands with which you can manage and arrange your files in whatever fashion you desire.

It is very important to remember that when you give a filename as an argument to a UNIX command, the filename can be either a relative or absolute path to the file. If you give just the name of the file, you are specifying a file in the current directory. If you give a partial path to the file (as in `../<filename>`, or `<directoryname>/<filename>`) you are specifying a relative path. Finally, you can always give the absolute path from the / directory to the file. Following is a quick review of this lesson:

- The `touch` command sets the modification date of the file to the current time. This has the effect of creating new empty files if you need them.

- The `rm` command removes files. Use the `rm -i` option until you are quite certain that you know what you are doing, and then keep using it for a while longer. Recursive `rm` running in non-interactive mode can wipe your entire disk.

- The `cp` command copies one or more files. Although a slight oversimplification, it's easiest to remember that if you start with a single file, your destination needs to be a single file; if you start with multiple files, your destination must be something that can hold multiple files (such as a directory). You can also copy a single file to a directory if you want to.

- The mv command works a lot like cp, only it renames or moves files. The mv command cannot move directories across physical hardware boundaries, so every now and then UNIX's hardware abstraction fails with this command. If this happens, look to the cp command for help.

- The ln command creates alternative names by which a file or directory can be accessed. It's convenient for times when you need one thing to appear to be in several different places, or when you need to make information that comes from different files at different times all appear as the same filename.

LESSON 7
READING FILES

In this lesson you will learn about several utilities that enable you to view portions—or the full contents—of text files.

Your UNIX machine can be used for hundreds of applications; no matter what the use, however, you're going to need to know how to do one very simple task: read files. Most UNIX applications use simple text-based configuration files, come with text-based instruction files, and store text-based log files. Undoubtedly, you're going to want to tap into this information. Other than loading up a text-editor or word processor, how can you do this? This lesson answers that question by showing you several quick-n-dirty commands that enable you to see what's inside all those files on your computer.

CONCATENATING FILES: cat

The simplest way to look at files is to use cat, the *concatenate* command. This might seem a bit strange because concatenate generally refers to the process of adding something onto something else. cat actually does just that—it concatenates all the data you provide and then hands it back to you. What happens if you supply more than one filename to the command? It displays the contents of all the files for which it is given names, one immediately after another. You can use cat along with a redirection operator (you'll learn about those in Lesson 12, "Input and Output") to create one file that holds the contents of several other files. For now, though, you'll use cat to display a file.

To display a file, just supply cat with the file or files you want to show as arguments to the command.

For example, suppose you have two files, one named kiwi.txt that contains the text "Kiwis are small, brown, and fuzzy," and another file called food.txt that holds "They are good to eat." Let's see what happens when you cat them.

```
>cat kiwi.txt food.txt
Kiwis are small, brown, and fuzzy.
They are good to eat.
```

The contents of the two files are displayed on the screen, one after the other. Pretty easy, huh? The biggest problem you'll have with cat is that files scroll off the screen if they are too large—but you're about to learn a way around that.

 UNIX Shortcut   If you want to display all the files ending in .txt in the directory, you can use wildcards with any of the commands discussed in this lesson. The command cat *.txt shows everything that ends with .txt in the current directory.

VIEWING A PAGE AT A TIME: PAGERS

The cat command is fine when you just want to quickly show some information—but what about large files that scroll past a bit too quickly to read? Luckily, there are some utilities specifically created for reading files from the command line: more, and the more recent and more powerful less. These are often referred to by the generic term *pagers*, as they display files to your window or screen one page at a time.

THE EVERPRESENT PAGER: more

Like cat, to use more all you need to do is type the command followed by the file or files you want to display.

For example, type

```
>more longfile.txt
```

This displays the file longfile.txt using more. Showing the output of the command is a waste of space because the results are simply the contents of the file, shown one page at a time. Instead, following are some commands you can use from within more to control the process:

- **Spacebar**—Advances the output to the next page.

- **q**—Quits out of the more program, exiting to the command line.

- **s**—Skips forward one line in the file. Use this to slowly advance through the file.

- **f**—Skips an entire page in the file.

- **/<pattern>**—Search and jump to a pattern or word in the file.

- **?** or **h**—Displays help for the more command. Because you can use this while viewing a file, it's probably the most important one to remember.

more is probably available on any UNIX computer that you happen to use. If you're lucky, your system might include—or your system support staff might have been kind enough to install—less. Believe it or not, less is more than more.

THE PAGER WITH MORE: **less**

less provides one important capability that some versions of more lack—the ability to move backwards through files. Once again, invoking less is identical to using cat and more. Just supply the files you want to view as arguments to the command.

For example

>less longfile.txt

As with more, less displays longfile.txt one page at a time. Controlling the output from less is very similar to more. There are several commands that enable you to move around within less:

- **Spacebar**—Advances the output to the next page.

- **b**—Backs up one page.

- **q**—Quits out of the less program, exiting to the command line.

- **Up arrow** (or **k**)—Scroll up one line.

- **Down arrow** (or **j**)—Scroll down one line.

- **/<pattern>**—Search forward and jump to a pattern or word in the file.

- **?<*pattern*>**—Search backwards and jump to a pattern or word in the file.

- **h**—Displays help for the `less` command.

Please keep in mind that this is not meant to be a comprehensive list of all the options that `more` and `less` support. In fact, if this book were to include all the options you can use with less, it would probably occupy 20 pages. What is included here is meant to give you enough information to get started.

PEEKING AT PARTS OF A FILE

There are some instances when you're only interested in what is stored at the top or bottom of a file. Although it might initially sound odd, if you spend much time using UNIX you'll find that these are very useful tricks. Suppose you have a directory filled with saved email or newsgroup messages. Rather than displaying each message in its entirety you might just want to see the header of the message, which contains the subject and sender address. To do this, use the `head` command to show you the beginning of the file. Similarly, if you're running a Web server and want to see the last few people who accessed your site, you can use `tail` to look at the end of your log file.

VIEWING THE BEGINNING: head

You might be noticing a common thread between all the programs we've looked at. To run them, all you need to do is supply the command followed by the file or files you want to view. The same continues to hold true for `head`. By default, `head` displays the first ten lines of each file you specify.

For example

```
>head news112.msg
From ksteinmetz@nwu.edu Mon Mar  4 13:11:12 PST 1998
Article: 28223 of comp.sys.next.sysadmin
Path: magnus.acs.ohio-state.edu!math.ohio-state.edu!
➥newsfeed.acns.nwu.edu!news.acns.nwu.edu!news
From: ksteinmetz@nwu.edu (Kimberly A. Steinmetz)
Newsgroups: comp.sys.next.sysadmin
```

```
Subject: Re: Q: Booting lockup? How to solve?
Date: 3 Mar 1996 18:23:32 GMT
Organization: Northwestern University, Evanston, IL, US
Lines: 44
Message-ID: <4hco34$o26@news.acns.nwu.edu>
```

In this example, the first ten lines of the file news112.msg are displayed. If you'd like to change the number of lines that are displayed, use the option **-#**, where # is the number of lines you'd like to view.

VIEWING THE END: `tail`

Tail is the inverse of `head`. Instead of displaying files from the start of a file, `tail` shows what is at the end of a file. Because most logs grow by adding things to the end, `tail` is a very nice way to see the latest additions to any log.

For example

```
>tail /var/log/httpd/access_log
204.123.9.20 - - [28/Nov/1998:00:52:40 -0500] "GET
➥/lifetime/lt2-1e.html HTTP/1.0" 200 3398
204.123.9.20 - - [28/Nov/1998:00:52:40 -0500] "GET
➥/lifetime/lt1-2a.html HTTP/1.0" 200 3561
204.123.9.20 - - [28/Nov/1998:00:52:41 -0500] "GET
➥/enviro/fa97/enviro_5.html HTTP/1.0" 200 3839
204.123.9.20 - - [28/Nov/1998:00:52:41 -0500] "GET
➥/enviro/fa97/enviro_4.html HTTP/1.0" 200 3972
204.123.9.20 - - [28/Nov/1998:00:52:42 -0500] "GET
➥/b865/b865_01.html HTTP/1.0" 200 15368
204.123.9.20 - - [28/Nov/1998:00:52:42 -0500] "GET
➥/agf-fact/agf-125.html HTTP/1.0" 200 13540
204.123.9.20 - - [28/Nov/1998:00:52:43 -0500] "GET
➥/aex-fact/463.html HTTP/1.0" 404 170
204.123.9.20 - - [28/Nov/1998:00:52:43 -0500] "GET
➥/aex-fact/480_76.html HTTP/1.0" 404 173
204.123.9.20 - - [28/Nov/1998:00:52:43 -0500] "GET
➥/hyg-fact/3000/3019.html HTTP/1.0" 200 8127
216.106.18.176 - - [28/Nov/1998:00:52:55 -0500] "GET
➥/ HTTP/1.1" 200 15679
```

The last ten entries from the Web server log are displayed. Because the log file is around 50MB in size, it's a good thing you don't have to read through it with `cat` or `more` just to see what's at the bottom! You can change the number of lines that `tail` displays by using the -# option just as you do with head.

WATCHING FILES GROW: `tail -f`

An extremely useful feature of `tail` is the ability to show files as they grow, rather than just showing the end of a file and exiting. Using the `-f` (follow) option with `tail` will open a file, display the last ten lines, and start monitoring the file for new information. When a new line of data is written to the file, it is immediately displayed on the screen. To interactively monitor the Web server log from the previous example, use `tail -f` `/var/log/httpd/access_log`, and you will see hits on your Web server as they occur. (This presumes, of course, that your machine is running a Web server, and that its log is stored in /var/log/httpd/access_log.) Pressing **Ctrl+c** exits out of this `tail` mode.

OTHER FILE FORMATS

Besides text files, you might encounter other documentation and README file formats on your UNIX computer that you need to look at. Following is a brief summary of what you might encounter, listed by the filename extensions they are likely to have:

- **.Z**—A UNIX *compressed* file. To look at the contents of one of these files, you need to either uncompress it using the cleverly named `uncompress` command, or view it directly by using the `zcat` command.

- **.gz**—This is a gzipped, short for *gnu-zipped*, file. (Zip is a compression format.) Some documentation might come stored in this format. Rather than un-gzipping, or rather *gunzipping*, the file (`gunzip` is the program which actually expands the file), you can use `gzcat` to display the file directly.

- **.ps, .eps**—These are Postscript files. If you look at these files you'll notice that you can read the contents, but there is a lot of extraneous formatting information. Check out the `ghostscript` (or `gs`) command, the `ghostview` command, or the `xpsview` command if you need to view a Postscript file.

- **.html**—HTML files, obviously! If you aren't running the X Window System, you can read HTML files from the command line with the *lynx* Web browser. If you are running the X Window System, just load the file up in your Web browser.

- **.tex**—A TeX formatted file. *TeX* is a page layout language that is sometimes used to store program documentation. Look to the tex program, or the latex program, to work with these files.

- **.dvi**—The result of a TeX formatted file, somewhere between the markup language and the actual paper output. DVI actually is intended to be a *device independent* file which allows for similar display of marked up data on any platform. To view a dvi file, try the xdvi program if you're running the X Window System, dvips or dvi2ps if you'd like to print the documentation, or dvi2tty if you're stuck on a text-only terminal.

That covers most of the cases that you'll encounter. If you run into a file format that doesn't appear to be included here, look around for an accompanying README.TXT, or README.1ST file—these are likely to contain information on how to make use of the unknown files.

SUMMARY

Your UNIX computer is likely to be populated with a large number of documentation files, and more documentation comes with every new piece of software. This lesson should have given you a clear picture of the many different ways you can display files, or portions of files. Here's a review:

- **cat**—The concatenate command displays all the files you specify, one after the other. It does not pause at the end of pages.

- **more/less**—**more** and **less** are known as pagers. They page through their input files, one screen at a time. less offers the ability to scroll backwards through files, unlike more, which provides forward-only viewing.

- **head**—Displays the first few lines of a file. This is useful when you're trying to look at header information in files such as email messages.

- **tail**—Views the end of a file. Used with the -f option, tail provides the very useful capability of displaying a logfile as it is generated. Rather than each program needing its own monitoring utility, tail -f can be used instead.

- **Other file formats**—Although many UNIX information files are text- or HTML-based, there are other formats that you might encounter. This lesson looked briefly at some of those formats, and the programs that you can use to work with them.

LESSON 8
TEXT EDITING

In this lesson you will learn the basics of editing files in the UNIX environment.

As I pointed out in Lesson 7, "Reading Files," when using UNIX you are frequently required to work with text files. Now that you know how to read them, it's time to learn how to create and edit them. In this lesson, you will learn to start and exit the most common editors, perform simple insertions and deletions, and save your work.

Many UNIX programs use text files as input, create text files as output, or are configured commands and variables set up in a text file. In order to change the contents of these files you need to make use of a text editor.

As a matter of fact, most UNIX software doesn't know the difference between a text file and any other file. From the operating system's point of view, files are files are files. If the user chooses to view some of them as containing text and others as containing programs, that's the user's business. An interesting consequence of this lack of concern about a file's contents is that the operating system is just as happy to allow you to use a text editor to edit the contents of your spreadsheet program as it is to enable you to attempt to run your email. Of course, if you actually have execute permission set on your email and try to run it, it's almost certain to just segmentation-fault—crash—immediately; but UNIX will try.

 Editing to Your Advantage   If you are a programmer, you might find this lack of a distinction to be useful. On occasion, you might find a program that needs a minor change, such as correction of a misspelling or a

> change of wording. In this instance, it is sometimes most convenient to simply load the executable file into a text editor and make the correction directly in the binary. This isn't a trick for the faint of heart, but sometimes it's the quick fix you need...and sometimes it's the only fix for software that you don't have the source code for.

If you spend much time discussing UNIX editors with long-time UNIX users, you'll find that there is a disagreement of warlike proportions between the users of the two most common editors—vi and emacs. Although these editors are actually rather complimentary in their functions and are both useful tools to have in your toolbox, chances are you'll end up running into many users who insist that one or the other editor is completely useless. If you listen to them, you'll be depriving yourself of the better solution to some tasks.

Most UNIX editors have immense power. emacs, for example, not only contains its own built-in programming language, but can also function as a complete windowing system for users who are stuck on text-only terminals. However, there is not enough room in this quick guide to cover more than the basics. After mastering the simple tasks presented here, the interested reader can make a trip to the library or bookstore and choose from among the several books available on each of the more popular UNIX editors.

QUICK AND DIRTY EDITING: vi

The vi editor is UNIX's most universal editor. Some users pronounce it *vee-eye*, whereas others pronounce it *vye*. (There seems to be no consensus, but the people who call it vye are still wrong!) vi isn't an easy editor, and it isn't a friendly editor. What it is, however, is a quick-starting editor with a very small memory footprint, which you will find on every UNIX machine that you sit down in front of. Because of its ubiquity, knowing the basics of vi will enable you to work with your files even if there are no more-convenient editors available.

Follow these steps if you need to use vi:

1. Determine what file you want to edit.

2. Issue the vi command as **vi <filename>.** The vi editor can also be started with no filename if you'd prefer to start a new document and haven't decided on a name.

When you start vi there are a number of things you need to know to make it useful. The Return key has been included here because although some of these commands take effect immediately upon pressing the respective keys, others require Return to be pressed after them.

vi operates in one of two modes: command mode or insert mode. In command mode, you have control of things such as cursor position, deleting characters, and saving files. In insert mode, you can insert characters. This distinction is bound to be confusing at first, but you'll find that vi's speed and universal presence outweigh its odd interface when performing some tasks. Some of the most-used tasks are featured in Table 8.1.

TABLE 8.1   COMMON vi ACTIONS

MODE	KEY(S)/KEY COMBINATION(S)	ACTION
Command	l	Move right
	h	Move left
	j	Move to the next line
	k	Move to the previous line
	Put cursor on the character to delete and then hit the **x** key	Delete a character

continues

TABLE 8.1   CONTINUED

MODE	KEY(S)/KEY COMBINATION(S)	ACTION
	Press the **d** key twice	Delete an entire line (including to delete an empty line)
	Position cursor on the line to append and hit **A**	Append the end of a line
	i (before the character under the cursor) or **a** (after the character under the cursor)	Changes to insert mode
	:w Return	Save the file
	:w<filename>	Save the file to a new name
	:q Return	To exit vi
	:q! Return	Quit without saving
Insert mode	**Esc** key	Changes to command
	Backspace and **Delete** keys	Backspaces or deletes, but only for data just inserted

Because it is impossible to walk through a step-by-step example, try typing the following example; remember to compare what you're typing, refer to the preceding list of commands, and see what happens. Although the finer details are not revealed by this example, you will pick up enough to at least enable you to do useful work, and to get you out of any sticky vi situations you get yourself into.

Try typing the following exactly as it appears here and see what happens. Where a new line appears in the text, hit **Return**. Remember that **Esc** is the escape key.

```
> vi mynewfile
iThis is my new file
This is line one of my new file
This is a test
This is line four of my new file<esc>kddkA
This is line three of my new file<esc>
➥khhhhhhhhhhhhhhhhhhxxxitwo<esc>:wq!
```

Your machine will respond:

```
"mynewfile" [New file] 4 lines, 119 characters
```

Now, look at what you've got.

```
> cat mynewfile
This is my new file
This is line two of my new file
This is line three of my new file
This is line four of my new file
```

THE KING OF EDITORS: emacs

On the other end of the spectrum from vi's odd syntax and tiny footprint is emacs. In certain circles it is thought that *emacs* is an acronym for "emacs makes a computer slow" because emacs is certainly the editor of all editors. Including an email-reading client, a news-reading client, a programming language, an online help database, and a windowing system (to name only a few of its features), emacs can almost certainly do anything that you want an editor to do. With today's faster machines and nearly unlimited memory, emacs might even be able to work fast enough that you don't need a coffee break while it starts up.

From the point of view of the average user, emacs has a much more intuitive interface than vi. You're always in insert mode, and Control functions are handled by using Control+key sequences instead of a separate mode. To make use of emacs, you need to do the following:

1. Determine the name of the file you want to edit.

2. Issue the emacs command as **emacs <*filename*>**. The emacs editor can also be started without a filename if you want to create a new file.

After you've started emacs, you'll need to know some basics to make it useful. (But you hardly need the list that follows because emacs starts up by immediately giving you a list of ways to get help.) In the following list, whenever you see Ctrl+ preceding a character, it means that you need to hold down the Control key and type that character:

- The emacs editor doesn't have a separate mode for entering commands. You are always either typing a command or typing text— no switching modes between them. This is just like most word processors that you might be familiar with. To enter text, just type what you want to appear; to enter a command, just type the command (usually **Ctrl+someletter**, or **Esc x somecommand**).

- You can position the cursor keys in emacs by using the arrow-key keypad in most every version of emacs and terminal combination. If the arrow keys don't work, you can also position the cursor by using **Ctrl+f** to move forward, **Ctrl+b** to move backwards, **Ctrl+p** to move to the previous line, and **Ctrl+n** to move to the next line. Newer versions of emacs also enable you to position the cursor using the mouse, but many users actually find this less convenient than the cursor keys.

- You can delete everything from the cursor to the end of the current line by typing **Ctrl+k**.

- **Ctrl+g** is the emacs "quit what you're doing" command—if you've started typing a command and change your mind, use **Ctrl+g**.

- If you use **Ctrl+k** to delete a line or lines, you can type **Ctrl+y** to yank them back again.

- To save the file you're currently editing, type **Ctrl+x Ctrl+s**.

- To save the file to a new filename, type **Ctrl+x Ctrl+w** **<filename>Return**.

- To exit emacs type **Ctrl+x Ctrl+c**. If emacs proceeds to ask you about *unsaved buffers*, it's because you have unsaved work. You can either go back and save your work, or answer Yes to the "quit anyway?" question and go about your business.

COMMAND BASICS

Beyond the set of Ctrl+ commands available in emacs, there's also an amazingly extensible set of commands which come in to play if you use the escape key. These commands are usually known as emacs *meta* commands, even though the machine with the meta key from which they draw their name has long since faded into history. Although they're too complicated and too specific to cover in this book, access to many of the interesting emacs meta commands is accomplished by typing **Esc x**, and then typing a command of some sort, such as info, what-line, or goto-line. As a matter of fact, you can find many useful emacs commands by entering **Esc x** and then typing a few characters (that is, the beginning of what you think the command might be named), followed by a space. The editor then gives you a list of all commands with similar names; frequently, one that does what you want is on the list!

One useful meta command that you might want to try is as follows: start emacs, and then type **Esc+xhelp+Spacebar** (and a second space, if the first one just results in the *help* you typed being extended by a dash). This will bring up a list of emacs commands that start with *help*—including useful things such as "help-for-help," a very good place to start.

THE emacs TUTORIAL

Instead of a quick example for you to pick through, emacs provides its own help and tutorial functions. New users are always encouraged to take the emacs tutorial to introduce themselves to the features of the editor, and to learn how to ask it for help on other features.

To enter the emacs tutorial, all you need to do is start emacs, and type **Ctrl+hi** (hold the **Ctrl** key down, hit **h**, release the Ctrl key, and hit **i**). If you type a **?** after the **Ctrl+h**—instead of the **i**—you'll see that there's actually a whole world of alternatives to the **i**; these alternatives give you a large range of different types of helpful information. For now, take the tutorial. If you're curious, you can probably spend a few months exploring the other options.

DESKTOP ENVIRONMENT TOOLS: KDE'S BUILT-IN EDITOR

Many desktop environments, such as KDE, provide a very convenient point-and-click text editor with all the convenient mouse-based functionality you have probably come to expect from personal-computer editing programs.

To activate the KDE editor click on the **K** in the KDE toolbar. Now, choose **Applications** from the popup menu, and then **Editor** from its submenu. A window that looks like the one shown in Figure 8.1 will open.

FIGURE 8.1   The KDE desktop environment built-in editor.

Editor Patience   Sometimes it takes a few seconds for X Windows-based applications to start—and there's no spinning watch cursor to show you that the machine is actually doing what you asked it to. Don't worry if the editor doesn't open immediately. If you select the editor again before it opens, you'll eventually end up with two editors running.

The built-in KDE editor includes all the normal point-and-click selection, copying, insertion, and deletion features you might expect of a GUI-based editor. In addition, it uses KDE's abstraction of data location to allow things such as opening and saving files directly from Web-based URLs. In Figure 8.1, you can see that one of the KDE text editor menus is selected. Several of these convenient features are visible on the drop-down menu that has appeared.

Summary

In this lesson, you were introduced to the two most popular text editors on the UNIX platform: vi and emacs. It is best with both of these editors to learn by doing, and this lesson will provide you with the tools necessary to do the three most important tasks in a text editor: starting the editor, editing text, and exiting gracefully if you screw up. Because you know how to quit both vi and emacs without saving, don't be afraid to experiment. You also learned about KDE's built-in editor as a desktop environment alternative to the text-window based editors from the older UNIX world. Following is a review:

- The vi editor is fast and convenient for making small changes to files. It has a user interface that might be called *non-intuitive* at the kindest. The omnipresence of the vi editor, its speed of execution, and its small disk-space requirements make it a convenient choice for fast edits—and for when you're working at an unfamiliar machine.

- **Esc:q!** gets you out of vi in a hurry, and without saving any changes you've made.

- The emacs editor contains everything you need in an editor, and then some, and then some more. On older hardware, emacs was a very slow to start, very slow to respond editor, but this has been largely mitigated by today's fast machines and extremely inexpensive disk space and memory. Take the emacs tutorial, dig around in its info files (**Esc+xinfo+Return**), and find a book on emacs to read if you want to get the most out of this editor.

- **Ctrl+x Ctrl+c**, followed by answering Yes to any "quit anyway?" questions, gets you out of emacs in a hurry, and without saving any changes you've made.

LESSON 9
TEXT AND FILE UTILITIES

In this lesson you'll round out your look at text utilities by learning how to perform some routine, and some not-so-routine, tasks on text files.

Some of what you're going to see in this lesson might not seem to be useful, but using this information in conjunction with other commands can be very powerful. If you take up shell scripting (discussed in Lesson 14, "Basic Shell Scripting"), you'll appreciate that UNIX includes utilities that can make your programming life simpler.

COUNTING LINES, WORDS, AND CHARACTERS: wc

If you want to get quick statistics about a text file on your machine, but don't want to load it up into a word processor, you can use the wc command to provide information on the number of lines, words, and characters within a single file.

To use wc, simply supply the name of a file you want analyzed, in the following form: **wc <filename>**. If you pass more than one filename to wc, all the files are processed, and a grand total for everything is returned.

For example

```
>wc *.txt

    300    2799   16284 intro.txt
   4944   43494  257939 lesson7.txt
   5244   46293  274223 total
```

In this example, wc has processed all the .txt files in the current directory (intro.txt and lesson7.txt). Four columns of information are returned for each file. The first value is the number of lines in the file, the second is a count of the words in the file, and the third is the number of characters. The final column, of course, is the filename. If you want to limit the values to either lines, words, or characters, you can use the -l, -w, or -c options, respectively.

 Uses for wc   A common use for wc is to check the number of entries in log files. For example, to see how many hits a Web server has received since the last time the log files were reset, you can use a command such as wc -l /var/log/httpd/access_log. This returns the number of lines in the access_log file. Because each line represents a hit, you can use wc to quickly count the hits.

SORTING INFORMATION: sort

Sorting is another useful function that you can do quickly with a built-in command rather than writing a specialized utility to do it. For example, suppose you have a file called kiwi.txt that contains the following:

```
Joan   92
Will   78
John   21
Kim    99
Kama   05
Jack   07
```

It's pretty simple to sort these by hand (ignoring the numbers for now), but what if you have several thousand names instead of six? You can use the sort command. Let's try running sort on kiwi.txt and see what happens:

```
>sort kiwi.txt

Jack   07
Joan   92
John   21
Kama   05
Kim    99
Will   78
```

Everything is sorted as you might expect. Now, what if you want to sort by the number instead of by the name? To do this, you need to follow these steps:

1. Decide which column you want to sort by, and then inform sort of your decision by using **+*<columnnumber>*** as an argument to the command.

2. You also need to tell sort what character is separating the columns by using the -t option. In this case it's a few spaces, so you'd use -t" ".

3. Lastly, because there are a varying number of spaces between the name and number, you'll need to use *ignore blanks* option -b to tell sort to count a group of spaces as a single space.

For example

```
>sort +2 -t" " -b kiwi.txt
Kama   05
Jack   07
John   21
Will   78
Joan   92
Kim    99
```

Bingo! Exactly what you were hoping for, right? Now the file is sorted by the numbers in the second column. sort has many more options that you can explore on your own with the man pages, but you can see how it can be used to sort a variety of data stored in different formats.

CHOPPING UP FILES: split

Suppose you need to email a huge file to a friend, but their email system doesn't support receiving such large messages. Is it time to write a special splitting utility? Nope, it's already been done for you. The split command can cut a file into whatever length segments you want, based on the number of lines in a file or the bytes. Follow these steps to use split:

1. Choose your input file. For this example, I'm using kiwi.txt from the sort command.

2. Determine the number of lines you want stored in each output
file. You'll specify this by using **-l** *<number of lines>* as an
option to the **sort** command. If you prefer to use the number of
k or MB, you can use the -b option with k or m. For example: -l
3 divides a file into segments of three lines each; using -b 10k
results in segments 10k in size; and -b 10m creates 10 megabyte
segments.

3. Choose a base output filename for the results.

4. Invoke **sort** using the following syntax: **split** *
<inputfile> <outputfile>*.

For example

```
>split -l 3 kiwi.txt kiwisplit
>more kiwisplit*

::::::::::::::
kiwisplitaa
::::::::::::::
Joan   92
Will   78
John   21
::::::::::::::
kiwisplitab
::::::::::::::
Kim    99
Kama   05
Jack   07
```

The kiwi.txt file from the previous example has been run through split
and has been divided into two files of three lines each: kiwisplitaa and
kiwisplitab. I've displayed the contents of the files using the more command because split does not offer feedback upon completion.

After your files are split to a reasonable size, you can transmit them to the
pesky mailserver, or wherever else you want. This is just another example
of a built-in utility that will undoubtedly come in handy when you least
expect it.

REASSEMBLING SPLIT FILES: `cat`

So what do you do if you've got a bunch of split up files and want to put them back together? It's simple—remember the `cat` command? When you have a series of files named with something such as *<basename>* (*<basename>*aa, *<basename>*ab, *<basename>*ac...*<basename>*zz), you can reassemble them by issuing the `cat` command as follows: `cat <basename>* > complete.file`. After cat has concatenated the files for you, you can `mv` the complete.file (or whatever you named it) to whatever final name you want.

> **Working with Output Files** It's frequently best to call output files by names such as complete.file—something completely different than the *<basename>*—and then move them to their destination or final filename. This avoids potential confusion in those cases where you really want your final filename to be just *<basename>*.

COMPARING AND REVISING FILES: `diff` AND `patch`

You might be accustomed to creating documents and sending out revisions. Unfortunately, most of the time you probably have to send out complete copies of files when only a few words here and there have changed. In the UNIX community, there is a great deal of information exchange, and source code is passed back and forth constantly. Rather than always sending complete files, people rely on the `diff` and `patch` commands to only transfer whatever information has changed between revisions.

USING `diff`

The `diff` function takes two files—an original template file and an updated file—and produces an output *patchfile* that contains enough information to reconstruct the updated file given only the patchfile and the template file. Assume you have the original file templatefile.txt, which has the following contents:

```
Now is the time for all good
kiwis to come to the aid of
puppies.
```

You distribute this file among all your co-workers. (This is just an example, folks.) However, a few days later you update your wonderful file to a new file—updatedfile.txt—that looks like this:

```
Now is the time for all good and bad
kiwis to come to the aid of
puppies and children.
```

Rather than redistribute the new file (updatedfile.txt) to everyone, you can just make a patch that contains all the changes between the original file and the new file. To do this, use the diff command with the following syntax: **diff <template file> <updated file> > <patchfile>**. The patchfile can be any filename you want.

> **Redirecting Output**   The standalone > in this example is used to redirect output to a specific file, which you name. You can learn more about redirection in Lesson 12, "Input and Output."

For example

>diff templatefile.txt updatedfile.txt > patchfile.txt

The program will run and return you to a command line, with no messages. If you're interested in seeing what the patchfile contains, feel free to take a look at it with cat or more. In this example, the resulting patchfile is named patchfile.txt; distribute it to everyone who has the original templatefile.txt and needs to update it.

> **File Comparisons**   The diff command is also useful when you just want to know if two copies of the same file are identical or not. If you find yourself with multiple copies of similar files, diff is a fast way to find

> out whether they are identical and, if not, what
> changes have been made between them. If `diff` pro-
> duces no output, there are no differences between
> the files.

USING `patch`

Now the `patch` program comes into play. You invoke `patch` by simply
giving it the name of the file that you want to patch, followed by the name
of the patchfile.

For example

```
>patch templatefile.txt patchfile.txt
patching file `templatefile.txt'
```

That's all there is to it. The file templatefile.txt has now been updated and
is identical to the file updatedfile.txt. You can verify this by viewing tem-
platefile.txt:

```
>cat templatefile.txt
Now is the time for all good and bad
kiwis to come to the aid of
puppies and children.
```

If you looked at the patchfile, you might have noticed that it is about the
same size as updatedfile.txt; so, why not just distribute the entire file
instead of the patch? In the case of tiny files such as those used in this
example, it really doesn't make sense to create patches. If you're dealing
with files several thousand lines long that have one or two lines changed
somewhere in the middle, however, you'll find that `patch` and `diff` are
excellent ways to avoid sending gobs of redundant information.

Important Reminder   Always remember to keep a
copy of your template file around. In this example,
the patch was applied directly to the template file and
the template file was updated. If all further patches
are created from the updated file, no problem; however, if patches are created based on the original template, the templatefile.txt can no longer be patched.

SUMMARY

The commands you've just learned show you a bit of the power that is built into the UNIX operating system. You've probably seen utilities similar to this on other desktop systems, but they've been add-ons or pieces of commercial software. In the case of UNIX, it's all part of the operating system, and there's a whole lot more where this came from! Here's a review of what was learned in this lesson:

- **wc**—The wc command can provide quick character, line, and word counts for a single file or for a group of files.

- **sort**—sort enables you to sort information contained in separate lines within a textfile. It understands the notion of columns/fields of data, so you can use it to sort data in a variety of different formats.

- **split**—If you have files that are a bit too large to handle when sending email, writing to a floppy, and so on, you can use the split command to chop them up into smaller files. split can create files containing a certain number of lines, kilobytes, or megabytes.

- **diff/patch**—The combination of diff and patch enables you to distribute updates (to documents, source code, and so on) in an efficient manner. Rather than sending copies of entire updated files, you can use diff to create patchfiles that only contain the changes between one version of a file and the next.

LESSON 10

COMPRESSION AND ARCHIVING TOOLS

In this lesson, you will learn about the common UNIX tools for compressing and archiving files, as well as a few tools you can use to keep tabs on your disk usage.

Although conserving disk space has almost become a thing of the past, it is still occasionally necessary to compress your files or bundle them up for archival purposes.

COMPRESSING FILES

Historically, hard disk storage space has been an expensive commodity in both the corporate and home-use environments.

> **Times Sure Do Change** On a purely historical note, an 80Mb SCSI-1 drive cost $369 in 1988, and a 20Mb MFM replacement drive for a PC-AT recently found by a friend of the author included its original packing receipt—a bill to the tune of $720! Today, $500 can buy 5GB or more of storage.

With today's extremely inexpensive hard-drives, the pressure to maximize disk usage efficiency is much lower than it has been in the past; but in some environments, such as schools, the pressure is still present. If you happen to be using a system where disk space is at a premium, you can use the commands in the compression section of this lesson to reduce the amount of space your files occupy—or to fit more stuff in the space you are allowed. Even if disk space isn't a concern for you, there are occasions, such as when sending files via email or distributing them over the Internet, when compressing files might be a wise choice.

There are three major compression formats you are likely to encounter when using UNIX: *compressed* files made using the UNIX program com-press, *zipped* files made using UNIX or personal computer versions of the PKZIP program, and *gzipped* files made using the GNU gzip utility. Each of these formats has a set of programs for compressing and uncompressing. Also appearing recently is the bzip2 compression utility, which, despite being the new kid on the block, looks very promising for tight compression.

compress/uncompress/zcat

The creatively named compress command uses an older UNIX compression format that is slowly dying out as the gzip format gains popularity. Files created with the compress command have the file suffix .Z. To use the compress command to compress a file, you simply issue the command as **compress <filename>**.

The equally creatively named uncompress command uncompresses (surprise!) the results of a compress command. To use the uncompress command, you issue the command as **uncompress <filename.Z>**.

The zcat command (with its slightly less intuitive name) is a version of cat that reads compressed files rather than normal text files.

Using zcat is as intuitive as using compress and uncompress; issue the command as **zcat <filename.Z>**. To make zcat somewhat more useful if you're trying to look at a large file, you can *pipe* the output into your pager of preference. To do this, issue the command as **zcat <filename.Z> ¦ more**. The vertical bar, ¦, is the UNIX *pipe* character—it pipes the output of the command preceding it into the input of the command following it. (You'll learn more on this in Lesson 12, "Input and Output.")

For example, if you've got a compressed file named stuffed.Z and you want to read stuffed without bothering to uncompress it first, you can type:

```
> zcat stuffed.Z ¦ more
```

Your machine will respond by using more to page you through the document.

zip/unzip

Based on the algorithm from the PC standard PKZip program, the zip and unzip programs work exactly as you might expect them to: **zip <filename>** to compress a file with zip, and **unzip <filename.z>** to unzip the files.

Creating files using the zip format (which uses the file suffix .z in UNIX) for distribution to other UNIX users is generally not a good idea, as zip and unzip are not always available to UNIX users; these utilities are freeware, so get your system administrator to install them if you need to have access to them. If your target, however, is users of Macintosh or Windows computers, zip is a file format that they can most likely read.

Both the zip and unzip programs have a number of potentially useful options, a list of which can be displayed by issuing either command followed by the option -h.

gzip/gunzip/gzcat

gzip, the GNU free software answer to the compress/uncompress suite of programs, was created in response to the realization that UNIX's compress/uncompress programs were based on proprietary algorithms—and that this might someday entail licensing fees. Again, the gzip, gunzip and gzcat programs work essentially identically to the compress/uncompress/zcat suite. Files compressed in the gzip format use the file suffix .gz and are generally smaller than files compressed with compress.

To make your life a bit easier, GNU has included the capability to deal with compressed (.Z) files in their gunzip and gzcat utilities.

> You might find that gzip and gunzip exist on your system, but that gzcat is missing. Some distributions have renamed gzcat to zcat because it handles compressed files as well.

bzip2/bunzip2

Although it is a relatively new addition to the UNIX compression scene, the bzip2 compressor appears to produce better compression than either compress or gzip. The syntax and options for bzip2 have intentionally been made similar to gzip, so if you encounter this program as it grows in popularity, you won't have too much trouble figuring it out. Compression with bzip2 follows the gzip format **bzip2 *<filename>***, which produces the compressed file <filename.bz2>. Decompression is simply **bunzip2 *<filename.bz2>***.

The bzip2 compression and decompression utilities appear to be in development as of this writing, so it would not be surprising to find that the commands evolve over time (bzip2 and .bz2 files are an update of a prior bzip program which made .bz files). If you encounter these programs and need to do more than trivial compressions or decompressions, it is recommended that you consult your local man pages for more current information.

MANAGING YOUR DISK USAGE

If you're on a system where you need to worry about disk usage, have a disk quota which you must remain under, or are just curious about how much space your files are taking up, there are a number of ways for you to look at this data; they are detailed in the following list:

- **The ls command**   Referring back to Lesson 4, "The File System," you know that you can use the ls command with the -l option to display disk usage for a file or files. If you need to scan quickly through your files to see which ones are taking up the most room, this is a quick way to do it.

- **The find command**   In Lesson 5, "Finding Files," you were introduced to using the find command to find files larger than a certain size. Although similar in utility to the ls -l command for this purpose, find -size # is a faster way to collect information on all files larger than # kilobytes—you just have to know what # you're looking for.

- **The df command**   Used mostly by system administrator types, the df command gives information about disk usage. Depending on your version of UNIX, you might have to give df different options to get it to produce readable output; but the general form you'd be interested in is df ./, which asks the file system to tell you about the usage of the drive upon which the current directory resides. The response is usually in the form of a logical device name (which you can ignore), followed by information about the total capacity of the device, the amount of storage in use on the device, the percentage of usage of the device, and the *mount point* (path to the directory at which the device appears) for the device. You might have to try variations on df ./ or df -k ./, or check your man pages to find the option that works on your version of UNIX.

- **The du command**   Another system administrator type command, du provides information about disk usage by directory. Again, different versions of UNIX use slightly different syntaxes; the general form you will be most interested in is du -s *, which asks the file system to produce a disk usage summary for everything in the current directory. For each item in the current directory, du -s * returns a summary of the total disk space used by the contents of the files or directories. Depending on your version of UNIX, you might or might not need to supply du with the -k flag to convince it to show you the disk usage in values of kilobytes (otherwise it shows you the disk usage in values of the file system's native block-size—usually 512 bytes).

ARCHIVING FILES: tar

If you spend much time using UNIX systems, you're bound to run into tar files. *Tar* is short for *Tape Archive*, though the tar command and its output are rarely used for archiving to tape anymore. More sophisticated and more powerful programs have taken over the job of archiving to tape, but the tar command remains a convenient and useful tool for personal archiving and distribution of files.

The tar command in its simplest form either creates or unpacks archive files. When creating an archive, you provide tar with a filename for the archive and a list of files that you want to archive. The program then collects all the files and bundles them into a single *tar-file*, which you can then store for future use or distribute conveniently via the World Wide Web, FTP, or email. When unpacking archives, you provide `tar` with the name of a tar-file and it extracts the contents of the file into the current directory, with the exact same file names, paths, and contents that existed on the system where it was tarred.

To use tar to create an archive, use the following steps:

1. Determine the name you want for your archive tar-file; normally, it will have the suffix .tar.

2. Determine the filenames of all the files you want to include in the tar-file, or, more often, the name of a directory that you want to archive.

3. Issue the tar command as **tar -cvf <*tarfilename.tar*> <*files or directories*>**.

For example, if you have a directory named lots-a-stuff in the current directory, you can archive the entire contents of lots-a-stuff—all the files in it, and all the directories in it, and all the files in all the directories in it, and so on—by typing the following:

```
> tar -cvf lotsastuff.tar lots-a-stuff
```

Because you gave it the -v (or *verbose*) option, your machine responds by telling you about every file that it's putting in the archive; in the end you have a new file named lotsastuff.tar. This new file contains the entire contents of your lots-a-stuff directory, with all the directory structure and file attribute information intact.

To unpack a tar-file, you simply issue the command **tar -xvf <*tarfilename.tar*>**.

If you give this file to a friend, your friend can unpack the tar-file by typing the following:

```
> tar -xvf lotsastuff.tar
```

After a list of everything in the file (that -v option again), your friend has a new directory named lots-a-stuff in his or her current directory, and it contains the complete contents of your lots-a-stuff directory. Any subdirectories in your lots-a-stuff directory, as well as all their contents, are present.

Polite Use of `tar`   If you don't know what is in a tar-file, it's often a good idea to use `tar -tvf` `<tarfile.tar>` before unpacking it. The `-t` option is the *tell* option, and asks tar to tell you about the contents of the file rather than unpacking it. This is a useful way to determine if the person who created the tar-file was a nice person who put everything in a directory and then tarred the directory, or if they were an impolite person who put everything in the current directory before tarring it. If you run into a tar-file created by an impolite user and make the mistake of untarring it in an inconvenient place—your home directory, for example—`tar` will end up dribbling files all over your home directory. You will then be stuck finding all the files and putting them in a subdirectory by hand, which can sometimes be a very tedious process. Be a polite user—don't tar files, `tar` directories.

If you've accidentally untarred an unfriendly tar-file, you can remove it all again by automating the `rm` command. (You will learn more on this sort of automation in Lesson 14, "Basic Shell Scripting.") If you're brave enough to try this, the command `\rm -rf` `` `tar -tf <tarfile>` `` does the trick. However, until you're comfortable enough with UNIX to look up the parts of that command and understand what it does, it's not recommended that you experiment with this.

PREPARING FOR EMAIL TRANSMISSION: uuencode/uudecode

If you need to send your files to another user, you can do so easily by including them in an email message. Today's personal computers can all do this fairly transparently by using *attachments*, but UNIX users have been largely left behind. Email on UNIX machines pre-dates the existence of most personal computers, and UNIX users had been transferring files around the world in email for years before personal computers discovered the concept of the Internet. Many UNIX users, however, are still stuck making attachments by hand—which seems a little unfair because it's UNIX machines that do the work of making the Internet possible for the personal computer users. If you aren't using one of the more user-friendly email clients (more on email clients in Lesson 18, "Accessing the Network Resources") that can handle attachments automatically, you'll need to create them manually and insert them into your email yourself. Still, it isn't a very difficult task. The more difficult task is convincing the personal computer users you might have to interact with to use a cross-platform attachment format, such as uuencode, instead of whichever proprietary format the popmail-client authors decide to favor this week.

The uuencode program accepts any file as input, and it produces an encoding of the file that can be included in an email message. To a person, the contents of this file look like random characters; on the receiving end, however, the user can use the uudecode program to extract the original file. Because every email program is different, you'll need to consult the documentation for your email client on how to include a file in a message. Here, you'll just learn how to create the uuencoded file from your original, and how to uudecode it again on the other side.

To use the uuencode command, you need to follow these steps:

1. Determine the name of the file you want to encode for email transmission.

2. Determine what you want the file to call itself at the other end.

3. Issue the uuencode command as **uuencode *<filename>* *<callmethis>* > *<filename>*.uue**. (Yes, you need to type the > before the *<filename>*.uue argument.)

Your computer will then produce a file named <filename>.uue which contains the uuencoded version of the file.

For example, if you have a file named sendtojoe and you want to uuencode it, you can type the following:

```
> uuencode sendtojoe hijoe > joe.uue
```

Your computer produces a file named joe.uue, which when decoded by Joe is named hijoe and contains the contents of your sendtojoe file.

Now you can copy and paste, or include, or do whatever you need to do to insert the file you just created into an email message and send it wherever you want.

Of course, if you receive a uuencoded file, you need to know how to decode the file. Decoding a uuencoded file is also extremely simple; issue the uudecode command as **uudecode <*filename.uue*>**.

Your machine will produce a file in the current directory identical to the one originally uuencoded.

Clearing up .uue   The filename of the .uue file and the filename to which it will decode itself do not have to be the same. This is sometimes confusing. If you receive a file named kludge.uue, issue the uudecode kludge.uue command, and do not find a file named kludge in your directory, don't be alarmed. The uuencoded file contains the filename as well as the uuencoded file contents. To find out what the uudecoded file will be named, use the head command to look at the first few lines of the uuencoded file. The filename to which it will decode appears on the first line.

KDE ARCHIVING TOOLS

Desktop environments also now provide convenient drag-and-drop file compression and archiving tools. The KDE environment, for example, provides the KZip archive and compression tool.

To access the KZip tool, click the **K** on the KDE toolbar, choose **Utilities** from the pop-up menu and **Zip** from its submenu. A window similar to the one shown in Figure 10.1 will appear.

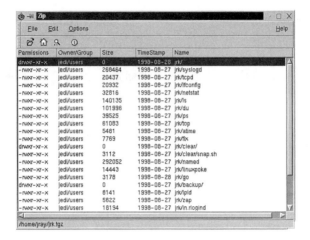

Figure 10.1 The KDE built-in archive manager, KZip.

The KDE KZip tool can work with `tar` and `gzip` files: choose **Open** from the **File** menu and select your archive. The KZip tool provides convenient features such as display of archive entry contents by simply double-clicking the entry, and drag-and-drop addition of files to archives.

SUMMARY

When you need to conserve disk space or shorten file transmission times, you might need to resort to compacting your files with some sort of compression utility. Here's a look at what was learned in this lesson:

- The three common compression utilities on UNIX systems are the omnipresent `compress`, the newer and smarter `gzip`, and the cross-platform `zip` programs. A relatively new addition to the UNIX compression scene is `bzip2`, which appears to produce better compression than `compress` or `gzip`.

- When you need to provide a collection of files to other users or simply archive a set of files for future use, you can use `tar` to create tar-files that contain all your files in one convenient package.

- Don't be an impolite user and use `tar` to archive individual files. Instead, put all the files you want to archive in a directory and `tar` the directory.

- If you need to send a file to someone via email, you can create an email-able encoding of the file by using the `uuencode` command.

- Don't be alarmed if you `uudecode` a file and can't immediately find it—the real filename is stored in plain text at the beginning of the file.

LESSON 11
PROCESSES

In this lesson you will learn how to work with processes: view them, kill them, and bend them to your whims!

Everything that you've run on your system in the previous lessons, and everything that you're going to be running in the rest of the lessons, created *processes* on your system. Each command creates a process that the UNIX operating system runs until it is finished or *killed*. Unlike some desktop operating systems, you can create processes that run entirely in the background, or that start and run in the middle of the night—without you even needing to be logged into the computer.

MORE THAN ONE COMMAND AT A TIME

UNIX enables you to run more than a single command at a time. This capability is known as *multi-tasking* and is available in different forms on some other operating systems as well. What makes UNIX different is that absolutely everything on UNIX is a process: Want a clock? Run a program. Need to copy files? That's a process too. Opening a window—yet another process. Although many personal computer OSes enable you to run a few applications at the same time, most handle large portions of their functionality by having it all be part of one big program. On UNIX, the actual operating system is very small, and it runs lots of programs simultaneously to provide the interface and other functionality to you.

Along with UNIX's absolute requirement to run many simultaneous programs just to provide the environment to the user comes the fact that the user can run as many simultaneous programs as he or she wants. On a UNIX box, you run programs for anything that you want to do. As a consequence of the way the OS works, it doesn't actually matter whether or not you're logged in while they run. Your being logged in is—you got it—just another process.

PUTTING A COMMAND INTO THE BACKGROUND: &

Making a command run in the background is simple; you simply add an &
to the end of the line containing the command.

For example, suppose you are running a program called analog to analyze
your Web server logfiles. Most log analysis takes quite some time for a
busy Web server, so you probably don't want to wait around for the command to finish. In order to run analog in the background, you can just
type the following:

```
>analog /var/log/httpd/access_log &

[3] 32566
>
```

The results are a bit cryptic, but you can see that you are returned to the
command line, ready to go about your business! The two numbers that are
returned identify the process on the system. The first result, [3], identifies
this as process number 3 that you've sent to the background. The second
number, 32566, is the process ID. Your UNIX system potentially has hundreds of processes running on it, and each one is assigned a unique number. Whatever number your process happens to be assigned is returned as
the second result value.

Running More than One Command   To run several
commands, one after the other, and put the whole
group into the background, you can use the following
syntax: (<command 1>;<command 2>;< command 3>) &.
This creates a new shell to execute the commands and
places it in the background. For example, if you
wanted to run the analog utility on two files, you
might use something such as the following:
`(analog/var/log/httpd/access_log; analog`
`/var/log/httpd/new_access_log) &`.

SUSPENDING A COMMAND AND MOVING IT TO THE BACKGROUND: CTRL+Z AND bg

If you happen to start a command without putting it into the background, you can still turn it into a background process. Let's assume you've started the analog command without the ampersand.

Following is an example:

```
>analog /var/log/httpd/access_log
```

To turn this into a background process, first press **Ctrl+z** to suspend the process. For example

```
Ctrl+z
[3]+  Stopped                    analog
➡/var/log/httpd/access_log
```

The analog command has now been suspended, and is assigned process number 3. Remember, this is not the same as the process ID. It identifies the process number locally in your session, not globally to the system.

To finish putting analog into the background, use the bg command followed by the local process number that you want to put into the background, as in **bg %<process number>**. In this example, analog is assigned the process number 3, so that's what you use in conjunction with bg. For example

```
>bg %3
[3]+ analog /var/log/httpd/access_log &
```

UNIX responds by showing you that analog is now running with the & in the background, and you can continue using the system.

 Using bg   If you issue the bg command without an argument, it puts the most recent job you've suspended into the background; so, here you might have gotten away with just bg.

RETURNING A PROCESS TO THE FOREGROUND: fg

What happens if a process is accidentally backgrounded, or if you want to return a process to the foreground so that you can manually control it or check its status? In this case, you'd use the command fg and the process number to return that process to the foreground, with the syntax **fg %<process number>**.

In the preceding example, the analog process was assigned the local process number 3 when it was put in the background. To bring it to the foreground, you'd type the following:

```
>fg %3
analog /var/log/httpd/access_log
```

You're now in complete control of the analog process again, as it is now running in the foreground.

 Missing Process Number?   What can you do if you've forgotten the local process number? Use the jobs command. The jobs command gives you a short listing of all your suspended and backgrounded processes, as well as their associated numbers.

LISTING THE RUNNING PROCESSES: ps

If you really start using the backgrounding capabilities of UNIX, at some point you're going to want to find out what you have running. To do this, you can use the ps command. The ps command returns a list of all the processes that you currently own.

For example

```
>ps
  PID TTY STAT   TIME COMMAND
 8832  p1 R     0:00 ps
30674  p1 S     0:00 /bin/login -h
➥NEW93114217.columbus.here.com -p
30675  p1 S     0:00 -bash
31136  p1 T     0:00 analog /var/log/httpd/access_log
```

> **Working with ps**   Don't be alarmed if your ps command doesn't return exactly these results. This is one of the places where different versions of UNIX have commands that are similar, but not identical. The ps command has many options for formatting its display, so you might want to take a look at the man page for your system.

If you run ps and see this result, it means that these are all the commands you currently have running. The columns are the system *process ID* (*PID*), the controlling terminal, the status of the process (running, sleeping, and so on), and the process itself. These are just the processes that *you* own. If you want to see everything anybody is running, try running **ps -ax**—this lists all the users' processes (-a) and all processes that don't have a controlling terminal (-x). If this doesn't work, then try **ps -ef** The ps command has a huge number of options that can return tons of information. Take a look at the man page for more information. The primary concern right now is that you can list what you have running on the system and get your process IDs.

KILLING A PROCESS: kill, kill, kill!

Killing might sound a bit harsh for ending a process, but it does sum up the result quite nicely. When you kill a process you stop whatever it is doing, no matter what. If you're editing a file, you risk losing the entire file if you kill the process instead of exiting out of the editor normally.

USING kill

Although the kill command is mainly used to stop processes, it can also be used to send signals to a process. SIGKILL is one such signal, but there are others that are less severe. Depending on the signal that you send, the process might reload its configuration files and reinitialize itself. This is extremely nice when you're running something such as a Web server and need to add a MIME-type or change some server option without shutting down the server. To see a list of the signals that you can send using kill, invoke the command with **kill -1**, as follows:

```
>kill -1
 1) SIGHUP        2) SIGINT        3) SIGQUIT       4) SIGILL
 5) SIGTRAP       6) SIGIOT        7) SIGBUS        8) SIGFPE
 9) SIGKILL      10) SIGUSR1      11) SIGSEGV      12) SIGUSR2
13) SIGPIPE      14) SIGALRM      15) SIGTERM      17) SIGCHLD
18) SIGCONT      19) SIGSTOP      20) SIGTSTP      21) SIGTTIN
22) SIGTTOU      23) SIGURG       24) SIGXCPU      25) SIGXFSZ
26) SIGVTALRM    27) SIGPROF      28) SIGWINCH     29) SIGIO
30) SIGPWR
```

Documentation for the software you run on your system often includes information on the signals to which it will respond. The most important signals you'll need are SIGHUP and SIGKILL. SIGHUP is the hang up signal and often forces a reload of configuration information for server processes. SIGKILL, on the other hand, forces the command to quit—no matter what. To send one of the signals, use **kill -*<signal number>* *<process ID>* *<process ID>* ....**

For example, to kill process number 31136, type the following:

```
>kill -9 31136
[2]+  Killed                    analog
➥/var/log/httpd/access_log
```

If you look at the process listing again, PID 31136 will be gone. You've successfully killed it! Check by typing the following:

```
>ps
  PID TTY STAT  TIME COMMAND
18303  p1 R     0:00 ps
30674  p1 S     0:00 /bin/login -h
➥NEW93114217.columbus.here.com -p
30675  p1 S     0:00 -bash
```

Sure enough, kill has done away with process number 31136, and ana-log is no longer running on the system.

EXITING A SHELL TO KILL A PROCESS

If you've backgrounded several processes, chances are you don't need to explicitly kill them when you log out of the system. The shell sends a SIGHUP signal to all the processes you've started, which will probably kill them. If you want to create a process that will not be killed when you exit your shell, you can do this with nohup.

PREVENTING DEATH: nohup

The nohup command can be prefixed to any other command to prevent it from being killed with the SIGHUP signal. For example, if you wanted to prevent your analog process from being killed when you exit the shell, run it as follows:

```
>nohup analog /var/log/httpd/access_log &
nohup: appending output to `nohup.out'
```

This runs your analog program in the background and prevents it from being killed when you exit your shell. The system also notes that any output that the command produces will be stored in a file called nohup.out.

PROCESS PRIORITY: nice AND renice

Processes that run on UNIX have different levels of priority. The amount of priority that a process is given can alter how long it takes to complete, as well as how long other processes on the system might take to run. Processes are given *chunks* of time on the computer's CPU. The level of priority determines how many of these chunks a certain process gets. It isn't very nice to run a computationally intensive task that doesn't need to be finished quickly and have it use up all the processor time on the computer.

Priority levels on UNIX range from 20 to -20, with the default level being 0. Although it might seem a bit backwards, -20 is actually the highest priority a process can have, and 20 is the lowest. To control process priority, use the nice and renice commands.

USING nice

nice is another command that is used as a prefix to the command that you want to run. The syntax for nice is **nice -<priority> <command>**. Continuing the analog example you've been using in this lesson, you're going to run analog at the lowest level priority possible. Analyzing log-files is not a high priority task—there is no sense in running it quickly.

> **nice**   The `nice` command is yet another example of slight variations between different commands with the same name. Some versions of `nice` use `-n <priority>` instead of `-<priority>`.

For example

```
>nice -20 analog /var/log/httpd/access_log &
```

This puts the `analog` command into the background and assigns it a priority level of 20. Remember, this is the lowest level priority that a process can have!

> **Changing Priorities**   Normal users can't set priorities below 0—only the root user can do this. You can think of it as follows: running the program without `nice` is as high priority as you can get, and you can use the `nice` command to make it nicer to other users.

USING `renice`

Suppose, however, that you've started a command with default priority that has been running for a day—for example, analyzing that big Web server log—and you have no idea when it's going to finish. You figure you might as well lower the priority, and therefore its use of machine resources, and allow it to finish whenever it decides to. You can use `renice` to change the priority of a command that is already running.

To do this, follow these steps:

1. First, you'll need to get a listing of your processes and make a note of the PID that you want to change.

2. Issue the **renice** command using this syntax: **renice** *<priority> <process ID>*.

For example

```
>ps
  PID TTY STAT  TIME COMMAND
 8832  p1 R    0:00 ps
30674  p1 S    0:00 /bin/login -h
➥NEW93114217.columbus.here.com -p
30675  p1 S    0:00 -bash
31136  p1 R    0:00 analog /var/log/httpd/access_log
```

If you want to change analog PID 31136 so that it is running with a lower priority, you can use the renice command in the following manner:

```
>renice +15 31136
31136: old priority 0, new priority 15
```

PID 31136 is now running with the priority 15, as opposed to the original priority 0.

 Super User Power   It is important to note that only the super user (root) has the capability to raise the priority of a running process. You can only lower the priority of a process—so don't lower a priority thinking you can raise it if it runs too slowly. After it's lowered, it's stuck there unless your system administrator fixes it for you.

CHECKING THE PROCESSES ON YOUR COMPUTER: top

Viewing the busy processes on your system is as simple as running the top command. top displays a continually updated list of processes, the amount of time they are using, and the process priority. To exit out of top press the UNIX break-sequence **Ctrl+c**.

Getting the Right Results   The break sequence is actually a function of your shell. If your shell is seriously misconfigured (this sometimes happens if you remotely log into a UNIX machine and it can't figure out what type of terminal you're using), pressing **Ctrl+c** might just display ^c on your screen. To fix this, you can try issuing the command: **stty** **intr** **Ctrl+c**.

The processes using the most CPU time are listed at the top of the display, as follows:

```
>top
  9:47pm up  2 days,  5:44,  2 users,  load average:
➡0.07, 0.02, 0.00
83 processes: 82 sleeping, 1 running, 0 zombie, 0 stopped
CPU states:  1.8% user,  4.8% system,  0.0% nice, 93.4% idle
Mem:   63100K av,  57324K used,   5776K free,
➡34064K shrd,   5316K buff
Swap: 128924K av,  0K used, 128924K free        36656K cached
PID USER PRI NI SIZE RSS SHARE STAT LIB%CPU%MEM TIME COMMAND
12448jray 15 0  740  740 556   R     0   6.5 1.1 0:01  top
12435root 0  0  692  692 528   S     0   0.1 1.0 0:00  in.
➡telnetd
1    root 0  0  412  412 344   S     0   0.0 0.6 0:02 init
2    root 0  0   0    0   0    SW    0   0.0 0.0 0:00 kflushd
3    root-12-12 0    0   0     SW<   0   0.0 0.0 0:00 kswapd
521  root 0  0  888  888 676   S     0   0.0 1.4 0:00
➡CGServer
498  root 0  0  316  316 260   S     0   0.0 0.5 0:00
➡mingetty
436  root 0  0  628  628 516   S     0   0.0 0.9 0:00
➡safe_mysqld
  ...
```

There's a ton of information returned, and, if you watch the display, it updates in real-time. You can see the percentage of CPU usage, memory, and lots of other goodies. For more information, view the man page for top.

SCHEDULING COMMANDS: at AND cron

With the capability to run processes in the background comes the ability to schedule processes to run at certain times—even when you're not logged into the computer. There are two ways to set up your UNIX computer to run a command at a certain time. Unfortunately, these might be disabled, depending on the level of control your administrator has chosen to implement. Allowing users to schedule commands for any time they want can be a bit dangerous. The two commands that you'll want to check out are crontab and at; they are described as follows:

- **cron**—Runs constantly on your system, and is probably already in use to run log rotation and various cleanup commands. You can create a personal crontab file that holds information about the interval that you want a command to run, and then use the **crontab <filename>** command to add your request to the system's crontab file. cron enables you to run commands in intervals as small as a second or as long as a year. With some UNIX versions you can use **crontab -e** to bring up your currently set crontab entries directly into an editor as well.

- **at**—Enables you to run a command once, rather than at a repeating interval. This is useful if there is a processor-intensive task that you want to run after business hours so that other tasks aren't affected.

Before you attempt to use either crontab or at, check with your system administrator. Scheduling processes blindly can affect other users and degrade system performance tremendously if inappropriate processes are scheduled to run simultaneously.

X WINDOWS PROCESSES

If you've been playing around in the X Window System, it is probably obvious that you can run multiple programs at a single time. Each of these programs runs with its own PID, just as you'd expect. Each of these programs is launched separately, so they are actually already sharing processor time—no one program is in the foreground or background. You can adjust the process priority from the command line, just as you do with any other program. Exiting X Windows kills all the active processes you are running.

SUMMARY

You've covered a lot of ground in this lesson. Understanding processes can be a bit difficult at first, but, depending on your use of the system, you might never need to do much more than put a process into the background. If you use KDE exclusively, you'll find that processes work exactly as you might expect on any desktop operating system. Following is a review of what was discussed in this lesson:

- **&**—The ampersand can be used to put a process into the background. You want to use this if you are going to be running something that takes a long time to complete, and that requires little or no user interaction.

- **bg/fg**—The bg and fg commands can be used to move processes to and from background or foreground operation.

- **ps**—To list all the processes that you are running on the system, use the ps command. You can also view processes that are controlled by other users, but you can't modify their priority or kill them (the processes, not the users).

- **kill**—This command is used to send a signal to a process. Normally this signal terminates the execution of the process. In other cases, it can cause a program to reread its configuration file or reinitialize itself.

- **nohup**—Exiting a shell sends a SIGHUP (hangup) signal to all the running processes in that shell. To enable a process to continue running even after you log off, use the nohup command.

- **nice/renice**—Every process on the computer has a priority that controls how much processor time a process gets in order to complete its task. Priorities range from -20 to 20, with the negative numbers being the higher priority.

- **top**—The command top shows the current top CPU-usage processes that are running on the system. The display continuously updates, so you can view how much CPU time new processes take as they are added to the system.

- **at/crontab**—You can schedule commands to run at certain times on your system by using the at and crontab functions. You will want to check with your system administrator and read the appropriate man pages before attempting to do so.

- **The X Window System (X Windows)**—Programs running under the X Window System all execute simultaneously. There is no need to worry about backgrounding or foregrounding processes manually. You can, however, adjust the priority of X Windows applications from the command line, just as you do with any other process.

LESSON 12

INPUT AND
OUTPUT

In this lesson you will learn how to manage UNIX process input and output and inter-process communication.

Now that you have learned a bit about working with UNIX and its filesystem and managing UNIX processes, it's time to start putting things together and exploring some of the true power of UNIX. In this lesson, you'll also learn about one of the fundamental tools which makes UNIX as useful as it is: inter-process communication by input and output redirection.

At the heart of what makes UNIX so much more powerful than average desktop operating systems is the simple—but amazingly effective—way in which it abstracts process input and output. To paraphrase the model on which UNIX bases input and output, you can imagine that UNIX thinks of user input to a program as a stream—a stream of information. Output from the program back to the user can be thought of in the same way. Furthermore, if the input to the program from the user is a stream of information, why should the operating system care whether a user, a file, or even another program is providing this stream? When you understand the model of input and output as simply being streams of data, you can immediately see that, from the operating system's point of view, the endpoints of these streams are immaterial. So long as the source of the input stream provides the information that the program needs, it does not matter where it comes from. Likewise, provided that the destination of the output stream "behaves like a user," the operating system has no reason to care where the output stream is actually going.

How does UNIX make this model available to the user? By providing the concept of input and output *redirection*.

REDIRECTION

To accommodate the user in its streams-of-information–based view of the
world, UNIX defines certain concepts to which programs must adhere.
Specifically, UNIX defines several *information connections* for every program and enables the user to manipulate the source and destination of
these connections.

STDIN

The *input connection* for a program is called *STDIN—standard input*. A
program can expect the incoming data stream from the user (or wherever)
to appear at STDIN.

When you interact with a command-line based program, the program is
reading the data you are entering from STDIN. If you prefer not to enter
the data by hand, you can put it in a file and redirect the file into the program's STDIN.

A program that you can use for an example is the `spell` program. The
`spell` command finds misspellings. Given input on its STDIN, `spell`
parses through it, checks the input against a dictionary, and returns any
misspellings it finds. Issued from the command line, you might type the
following:

```
> spell
  Now is the tyem for all good kiwis to
  come to thie ayde of some very good UNIX users
  Ctrl+d
```

Pressing **Ctrl+d** finishes the input, and `spell` gets to work, returning the
following:

```
tyem
thie
ayde
```

Each of the misspelled words is displayed, just as you might expect—not
a particularly useful program at first glance. The `spell` program, however,
doesn't care whether it was you typing the input or whether the input
came from a file.

Working with `spell`   Actually, it's more proper to think of the `spell` program as not caring whether the input comes from a file or from a user. The `spell` program was designed to work with input coming from a file or program; it just happens that because of the input/output model, it doesn't mind if the input comes from a user instead. Many programs you'll find on UNIX fall into the same category—they are designed to take input or provide output to or from other programs and files. Because it is only the input/output model that allows direct user interaction with the software, you might occasionally find the syntax with which some of these programs converse to be slightly odd. Just remember, they weren't really designed to talk to users.

Use your favorite text editor to create a two-line file containing the same text you typed previously, and then try `spell` by redirecting its STDIN. If you named your file reallydumbfile, you can run `spell` on it by typing the following:

```
> spell < reallydumbfile
```

```
tyem
thie
ayde
```

The < character directs the contents of the file to its right into the STDIN of the command to the left.

STDOUT

The *output connection* which UNIX provides for programs is called *STD-OUT—standard output*. Just as you can redirect STDIN from a file, if you want to send the output of a command to a file you can redirect STDOUT. The > character directs the STDOUT of the program to its left into the contents of the file to its right. For example, if you like looking at the contents of your Web server logfile, and you want to put the last 30 lines into a file named kiwis-logs so that you can edit them, you can use the following command:

```
> tail -30 /usr/local/httpd/logs/access_log > kiwis-logs
```

This example directs the shell to create the file kiwis-logs and to put the STDOUT from the `tail` command into it. If kiwis-logs already exists, the file is erased before the data is put into it.

If for some reason you collect the end of the logfile periodically, you might want to have a complete archive of it. You can direct the shell to append the data to the file rather than having it clear the file first. To do this, issue the command as follows:

```
> tail -30 /usr/local/httpd/logs/access_log >> kiwis-logs
```

The >> character pair appends the STDOUT of the program to its left into the file to its right.

Of course, you can combine these redirections; if you want to check your spelling and save the results in a file, you can return to your `spell` command by typing the following:

```
> spell < reallydumbfile > reallydumbspellings
```

STDERR

To make your life easier, UNIX actually has two different output streams of data that it defines for programs. The first, STDOUT, you have already learned about. The second, STDERR, is used to allow the program to provide error messages to the user. If the user is redirecting STDOUT and the program can only put errors on STDOUT, the user might never see the errors—they all go into the redirected file. Instead, programs can use STDERR for errors, and if the user has not redirected it they can still see error messages and warnings while STDOUT is headed into another file or program.

If you want to put STDERR into the same file in which you're storing STDOUT, use >& instead of > in the command; you can do so as follows:

```
> spell < reallydumbfile >& reallydumbspelling
```

Shell Variations   If you're using another shell, be aware that redirection is one of the places where syntax varies significantly. Check the man pages for the shell of your preference to learn more.

PIPES

Not only can UNIX redirect STDIN and STDOUT from and to files, but because these are data streams to UNIX it also provides the idea of *piping* these streams directly between different programs. With pipes you can use the STDOUT of one program directly as the STDIN of another.

To create a pipe in UNIX, you simply use a ¦ character between the programs on the command line.

Again, using an example is so much more illustrative than a lot of words. Take the example of your compulsive collecting of your Web server logfiles. If, instead of collecting them in files, you want to amuse and amaze all your friends by sending them the tail end of the file (using email is discussed in Lesson 18, "Accessing the Network Resources"), you can do so without saving it in a file by using the following command:

```
> tail -30 /usr/local/httpd/logs/access_log ¦ mail
```

Thus far, your repertoire of UNIX commands probably isn't large enough to make this a truly useful feature for you, but as you learn more about UNIX you will find it a powerful tool for simplifying your tasks.

For now, one way in which you can make this feature work for you is by piping things into pagers. For example, if you want to be able to page through the output of the ls command, you can pipe it into more. Try typing the following:

```
> ls -lRaF / ¦ more
```

You see a particularly long listing of files; if you don't eventually press **Crtl+c** to get out of this list, it can go on for days. Because this is really a complete recursive listing of your entire filesystem in long format, you're not going to want to use this particular ls command too often. But any time you want to page through an ls listing—or any other program output that flows off your screen—you can pipe it into more.

Watch future examples carefully because the pipe will appear in more useful contexts throughout the rest of the book.

SPLITTING A PIPE: THE tee COMMAND

On occasion, you might want to direct STDOUT to a file while continuing to send it down a pipe to another program. In such a case, you can use the tee command.

Consider the (increasingly tedious) example of collecting the tail of Web logs. If you aren't satisfied with just emailing it to your friends as in the previous example, you can use the tee command to save it to a file at the same time. Type the following:

```
> tail -30 /usr/local/httpd/logs/access_log ¦ tee kiwi_
➥logs ¦ mail friend@somewhere.com
```

This helps you out if you want to both save the tail of the file in kiwi_logs and send it to annoy your friend.

SUMMARY

In this lesson, you were introduced to the UNIX model of process input and output, and to the easy way in which UNIX enables the user to connect programs together to accomplish complex tasks. Here's a review of some of the key points:

- Every program has a STDIN, a STDOUT, and a STDERR. Not all programs use them for user interaction (programs such as PhotoShop just don't lend themselves to command-line control), but for the vast majority that do, these input and output connections can be manipulated.

- You can provide the input data that a program expects on STDIN by hand, from a file, or from another program.

- You can send the STDOUT and STDERR of a program into a file if you want to collect it for future use rather than viewing it as it is produced.

- You can pipe the STDOUT of one program into the STDIN of another.

- One immediately useful thing to do with pipes is to pipe the output of particularly verbose programs into a pager (more, less).

Lesson 13

Regular Expressions

In this lesson you will learn the basics behind regular expressions, and how to use them with the grep command.

Regular expressions are a wonderful thing—accept this statement as a fact as you read through this lesson and you'll be fine. *Regular expressions*, or *RE*s, are used in many programming languages and UNIX commands. They are a bit on the esoteric side, but are extremely important to understand nonetheless. Although in this lesson you'll be looking only at the command grep in conjunction with regular expressions, you can apply this knowledge to almost everything that uses regular expressions. Mastering regular expressions takes time; this lesson is rather short and serves only as an introduction to the topic.

Pattern Matching

Regular expressions are a method of specifying a pattern of characters that can then be matched against existing text. They can be used to locate information when you're not quite sure what you're looking for, or they can be used to perform extremely complex search and replace procedures. The *Perl* (*Practical Extraction and Report Language*) programming language uses regular expressions to a great extent and is considered one of the best—if not *the* best—languages for creating dynamic Web applications.

Specifying the Regular Expression in grep

The format for specifying the regular expression in grep is as follows:
grep <regular expression> <filename> <filename> .... Because this lesson uses grep as its example, familiarize yourself with this format. Other programs sometimes require that the regular expression be set off with / on either side of it; this is not the case with grep.

MATCHING SINGLE AND MULTIPLE CHARACTERS: . AND *

Given that a regular expression defines a method of matching, this section discusses some of the most common parts of a regular expression and how they can be used to match a sample pattern. For the examples, you're going to use a sample file called sample.txt (if you want to follow along, use your favorite text editor to create it now); it looks like this:

```
This is a test
Kim Steinmetz
(614) 555-0591
(615) 555-0000
"special stuff"
1998
1999
1800
1750
```

The period character (.) can be used to match any character. For example, just assume that you can't remember how to spell Kim's last name in the preceding file. There's a good chance you might get the *i* and *e* mixed up. In that case, you can use . as follows:

```
> grep "St..nmetz" sample.txt
Kim Steinmetz
```

The *St* and *nmetz* make up an obvious part of the regular expression— they match directly with the letters in the name *Steinmetz*. Because you weren't sure about the *i* and *e*, you simply replaced them with periods, and grep returned the line you wanted.

With * you can match any number of occurrences of a pattern or portion of a pattern. Suppose all you knew was that Kim's last name started with an *s* and ended with a *z*. In this case, you can use * in conjunction with . to match anything between an *s* and a *z*; type the following:

```
> grep "S.*z" sample.txt
Kim Steinmetz
```

Sure enough, that works well! You can pretty much forget how to spell her name now, huh?

Figuring Out * It is important to note that * will match any number of occurrences of a pattern, including zero. This means that the expression s.*z will happily match the string *Sz*. If your expression is turning up matches that you hadn't planned on, this might be the cause.

Use \ to set off a special character. Some characters are used by the shell, so they must be escaped by using \. You might want to use this in front of characters that might be special characters as well. In most cases, it doesn't hurt to use \ if you aren't sure. For example, the shell usually expects you to put double quotes (") around strings with spaces in them—it uses the double quote to group the words in the string. If you need to search through your file for lines containing double quotes, you can not grep for "; instead, use the following command:

```
> grep \" sample.txt
"special stuff"
```

Using the \ in front of the double quote tells the shell to not attempt to interpret the double quote normally as a surrounding character, but to instead simply pass it to the grep command for processing.

USING AND NEGATING RANGES IN A REGULAR EXPRESSION: [ ] AND ^

You've noticed that the sample.txt file you've been using has a few dates inside. Suppose you only want to match the years that fall in the 1700-1800's. To do this you can use a range, which is specified in a regular expression as follows: [*<starting point>-<ending point>*]. The starting and ending points can be numbers or ranges within the alphabet.

For example, type the following:

```
> grep "1[7-8][0-9]*" sample.txt
1800
1750
```

Your pattern here states that any valid matches must start with a 1 and be followed by a number in the range from 7 to 8, followed by one or several numbers in the range from 0 to 9. Ranges can help you pull certain values out of files. You can expand the capability of the range by applying the negation operator.

The character ^ *negates* a range if it is used at the start of the range specification. Negating a range will match the opposite of what the range matches.

For example, type the following:

```
> grep "1[^7-8][0-9]*" sample.txt
(614) 555-0591
(615) 555-0000
1998
1999
```

Notice that you now match anything that isn't in the 1700's or 1800's. You also match two phone numbers that, if you look at the third and subsequent characters, do indeed match the pattern you've specified.

Finding the Perfect Match   You'll notice that you've asked the grep command to match a 1, followed by something that's not in the range from 7 to 8, followed by something that's in the range from 0 to 9; you matched the pattern 14). You might initially be surprised because the) isn't in the range from 0 to 9. Remember that the * character asks grep to look for zero or more something — in this case you've matched the 1, one thing that's not 7 to 8, and zero things from 0 to 9. This is not quite the same as regular expression syntax as used by many shells. Consult the man pages for your shell to learn the different ways that shells handle regular expressions.

MATCHING THE START AND END OF A LINE: ^ (AGAIN) AND $

In order to uniquely match the years in the sample file, you can use the start-of-line and end-of-line regular expression characters to stop grep from matching the phone numbers. These characters are commonly called *anchors* because they anchor a pattern to the start or end of a line. Because 1998 and 1999 are both at the beginning of a line, this will be easy.

If ^ is used outside of a range, the ^ character matches the start of a line.

$ matches the end of a line. If your pattern falls at the end of a line, you can anchor it in this position with $.

For example, type the following:

```
>grep "^1[^7-8][0-9]*" sample.txt
     1998
1999
```

That's more like it. Only the two dates are returned, because they fall at the beginning of a line. The phone numbers no longer match because the portion that did match is not at the start of the line.

USES FOR REGULAR EXPRESSIONS

What you've just learned is only a very tiny subset of the regular expressions that you can generate. Regular expressions can be used in a wide variety of different applications. For example, sed, the *stream editor*, can replace patterns of text from a stream of text on the fly. (It's great for editing a STDOUT -> STDIN stream between two programs!) Being able to do a global regular expression search and replace on a thousand files—rather than editing each individually—is a thing of beauty. When you are using the shell you can also use a subset of the complete regular expression library to specify filenames for operations.

For example, if you have a group of files named test1, test2, test3, test4, and test5, and you want to copy files 3 through 5 to a new directory, you can use a regular expression such as the following:

```
>cp test[3-5] newdirectory
```

You'll need to consult the man pages for the shell you are running in order to determine which regular expressions it supports. The same goes for everything else that uses regular expressions. Unfortunately, even though REs themselves are pretty standard, the extent to which any individual application supports them is entirely up to that application. Perl, for example, is an application (and, in turn, is a complete programming environment) which makes extensive use of regular expressions.

With the growing popularity of the World Wide Web comes the need to process user supplied information quickly and reliably. Unfortunately, there is little control over what sort of information a user might submit on a form or other interactive Web document. If you intend to do Web programming, you will find that regular expressions are a lifesaver and can be used to extract data from a form and turn it into a usable format. If this sounds interesting to you, you might do well to look into the Perl programming language because it makes very strong use of regular expressions.

Summary

Regular expressions are an extremely flexible way of describing a pattern to be matched. Because many UNIX applications, including the shell, support regular expressions, it is important to develop a general understanding of how they work and what they are good for. Hopefully this lesson has provided this background for you. Here's a review:

- .—This matches any character. Use it whenever you aren't sure what character falls in a specific position.

- *—Using the * matches any number of occurrences of a specific pattern. You can use this in conjunction with . or ranges.

- \—Special characters need to be escaped using the \ character. If you need to use the quote character (") in a pattern, you'll have to escape it.

- **Ranges**—You can match ranges of numbers or letters to limit a pattern. Ranges are enclosed in [ ] characters. To negate a range, use ^ at the beginning of the range specification.

- ^/$—These two special characters match the beginning and end of a line, respectively. They are commonly referred to as anchors because they anchor a pattern to a specific place on a line.

- **Regular Expressions**—These are used in many UNIX programs, and can be an extremely powerful tool. Read the man pages for your shell and other utilities in order to determine the extent to which they support regular expressions.

LESSON 14
BASIC SHELL SCRIPTING

In this lesson you will learn a bit more of the magic behind automation and customization using shell scripts.

When you learned about pipes in Lesson 12, "Input and Output," you probably began to see a bit of what makes UNIX so powerful and configurable. What you probably didn't realize is that using a pipe is only the very beginning of what UNIX can do to customize and automate tasks. As you read through this lesson, you'll soon see that pipes are only the smallest tip of the iceberg.

Shell scripts are essentially little programs written in the language of the shell. If you're a user from the pre-windows days of the PC, you'll recognize shell scripts as being similar to BATCH files. Macintosh users, although not burdened with a command line in day-to-day life, will still see the similarity to the AppleScript and Frontier scripting languages. While anything larger than a few dozen lines of script would probably be better done in a language other than the shell, thinking of shell scripts as little programs does injustice to the flexibility and convenience that they provide the user.

GETTING A LOT FOR A LITTLE: SHELL SCRIPTS

You will usually create a shell script when you want to combine a set of actions that you routinely need to repeat into a single convenient action.

For example, you might in the habit of coming in to work and starting your day off by wasting a bit of time—sending all your coworkers an email message saying "Howdy Neighbor", firing off a print job to print out the most recent 100 hits to your personal Web page, opening an `xterm` and reading a few newsgroups, and so on. If you want to save yourself some time and keystrokes you can do this by writing a little shell script to do it all automatically. You might put it all in a file and name it something such as waste-time; that way, in the future you'd just have to come in to work and type *waste-time* to have your computer waste time for you automatically.

Another instance of using shell scripts, or shell scripting techniques, is with some commands that can be used to automate certain tasks directly in the shell—without having to be put in a file. This lesson will look primarily at these because they're easier to learn and more immediately useful. As you get more comfortable with UNIX, you'll naturally gravitate to the idea of just putting what you're typing in a file—and another shell script programmer will be born.

SHELL SCRIPT FILES

As mentioned previously, shell scripts are small-in-size programs written in the same language that you use to talk to the shell by hand. It only makes sense that you can do this with UNIX—remember the UNIX model of input and output? The shell really doesn't care whether it's you issuing commands to it or if the commands are coming from some other source, such as a file.

 Shell Variations   The examples in this section are designed for the csh or tcsh shells. If you're using a different shell, you'll need to consult the man pages for your shell to determine the correct syntax, change your default shell (see Lesson 15, "User Utilities," for the chsh program), or start a csh or tcsh shell by typing csh or tcsh.

As a quick introduction to the sort of thing you can do with a shell script file, take the preceding waste-time example. If you want to actually write a shell script to do exactly this, you need to combine a few of the tools you've seen so far with a few that you haven't yet seen. However, for your edification, here's what to do:

1. Determine the name of your Web server log; here, /usr/local/httpd/logs/access_log is assumed.

2. Determine your username. (You'd better know this one by this point!) For the purposes of this example, you're named bob, and your email address is bob@very.important.com.

3. Figure out how to send email to a bunch of people with one command. This sort of behavior is generally frowned upon unless it's for good reason, so for this example you'll just send yourself email.

4. Figure out how you read news. Here, the trn command is used.

5. Learn where the binary for your shell is. If you're using csh, which csh. /bin/csh is assumed here.

6. Figure out how to print on your system. This example assumes you're on a system blessed with lpr.

7. Create the shell script file: vi waste-time.

8. Add the following lines to the shell script file:

```
#!/bin/csh
echo "Howdy Neighbor" ¦ mail bob@very.important.com
grep "bob" /usr/local/httpd/logs/access_log ¦
➡tail -100 ¦ lpr
xterm -e trn &
exit
```

9. Save the file and exit your editor. In vi, use :wq!Return.

10. Change the file attributes on the file so that you can execute it: chmod 755 waste-time.

11. Execute your new shell script: ./waste-time.

Caution!   You might or might not be able to use simply waste-time, instead of ./waste-time, depending on if the current directory is in your PATH environment variable (echo $PATH to check) or not.

Your script will, if everything works, produce exactly the results which were outlined at the beginning of this section.

To explain a few of the things that happened in this shell script, the following might be helpful—most of this will be understandable from what you've learned thus far:

- **echo**—This command puts things on its STDOUT. Here it is used to create a STDOUT stream containing "Howdy Neighbor," which is then fed to the mail STDIN via a pipe.

- **mail**—This command can take a message on STDIN and send it to a list of recipients. (mail is discussed in Lesson 18, "Accessing the Network Resources.")

- **grep**—You know what grep does, and what tail does. After the last 100 lines matching bob have been found, they're handed to lpr on its STDIN. lpr sends data to a printer. (lpr is discussed in Lesson 17, "Printing.")

- **xterm**—Starts a terminal, and can be told to start a program running in the terminal window by using the -e option.

So Many Shells on the Beach

As has probably become apparent to you if you've spent as much time playing with your UNIX account as you have reading this book, UNIX has an abundance of shells available for you to use. The syntax and available commands in each of these shells ranges from subtly different to extremely different. For the purposes of this lesson, you'll be using commands and syntax compatible with csh and tcsh.

The bourne shell, sh is probably the best shell to write scripts in if you're concerned about distributing large sophisticated scripts to unknown users. It's not the easiest shell to use at the command line, though, so you're better off starting with the same shell you use in day-to-day life.

Doing it Again and Again: foreach

Instead of spending time collecting commands into a file to automate them, you can get a lot of mileage out of simple automation techniques that don't involve putting commands in files at all. One of the commands used for this is the `foreach` command.

EXECUTING A COMMAND OVER AND OVER

If you find yourself in a situation where you need to repeatedly execute some action for each file in a set of files, the `foreach` command can help. It takes a list of files, and does something "for each" of them. The use is much easier to demonstrate than to explain. If you have a list of files that you need to do something to, you can follow these steps to use `foreach`:

1. Figure out what you want to do. In this example, you've got a bunch of directories, and you want to create a tarfile of each.

2. Decide on the names of the files/directories that you want to do your something to. In this case, you're going create tarfiles for the directories mydirectory, yourdirectory, and herdirectory.

3. Pick a variable name that you want to use; here you're just going to use a variable named `test`. It doesn't much matter what the variable name is, just so long as it doesn't conflict with the name of the command.

4. Issue the **foreach** command as **foreach** *`<variablename>`* (*`<filenames>`*). The `foreach` command then asks you what you want to do for each file by displaying a question mark. Fill this in with whatever you need to do. Again, you're going to be tarring files in the example. After giving `foreach` the command for whatever it is you want to do, finish it by putting the command end on a line by itself.

To illustrate the example, type the following:

```
> foreach test (mydirectory yourdirectory herdirectory)
? tar -cvf $test.tar $test
? end
```

Your machine responds by running the `tar` command for each file you gave it to work with. Inside the `foreach` command loop, note the use of the expression *$test*. `foreach` goes through the list of filenames you gave it and puts each one sequentially in the test variable. To use the contents of a variable in the shell, put a $ sign before it. For example, `foreach` first puts mydirectory in the variable test. It then runs the `tar` command, and the shell expands the test variable to mydirectory. The `tar` command that gets executed actually looks like the following: `tar -cvf mydirectory.tar mydirectory`. The next time through the loop, `foreach` puts yourdirectory in the variable test, and the process is repeated.

You can use regular expressions in the shell instead of enumerating the filenames to use the `foreach` command. If you notice in the previous example, all the directories you want to `tar` actually have part of their names in common—*directory*, in this instance. If you wanted to produce the same results without having to enumerate all the directory names to `foreach`, you might issue the preceding `foreach` command as follows: `foreach test (*directory)`. You can use the pattern matching tools you learned about in Lesson 13, "Regular Expressions," to match any collection of filenames you want.

RENAMING MULTIPLE FILES

You've probably noticed that the `mv` command can't do some really convenient things, such as renaming multiple files with new names instead of new locations; this is an ideal problem for `foreach`.

For example, imagine you have a bunch of files for a pet project, and they're named things such as brokenjunk.start, brokenjunk.today, brokenjunk.gif, and so on. Suddenly your boss decides that it's important that you give these files to the development department because they want to demo your project next week. This never happens to you, right? If it did, you might want to rename your files to something a little more professional. Instead of renaming the files one by one, you can use the `foreach` command to automate the task for you. In this case you might type the following:

```
> foreach test (brokenjunk.*)
? mv $test importantstuff.$test:e
? end
```

The part of this you might not immediately understand is the `$test:e` part. This says, "Expand the `$test` variable and toss out everything except for the stuff after the last . in the filename"—in this case, the parts that make the files different (*start*, *today*, and so on).

Of course, this isn't a very useful command for three files, but if you've got a project with hundreds of files it can save you a lot of typing.

MODIFYING AND REPLACING ORIGINALS

Another useful trick for which you can use the `foreach` command is when you need to apply a process to each of many files—and you want to do it without creating new files, instead just replacing the old ones in-place.

Say you have a collection of image files, each of which have a border which you want to crop off, and then you want to scale them to a smaller size. If the imaginary command `crop` took files on STDIN and wrote its data to STDOUT, you might use the `foreach` command similar to the following:

```
> foreach test (*.gif)
? crop < $test > holding
? mv holding $test
? end
```

Why not just do **crop < $test > $test**? Because you can't be guaranteed to get away with writing to the file while you're still reading from it—so you store the results in a temporary file named holding. Follow up by using the `mv` command to move the temporary file back to the original filename.

DOING IT AFTER A WHILE: `sleep`

The utility of a command that just sits there for a while is perhaps not readily apparent, but you will find uses when you have actions you want to repeat at relatively short intervals. If you do run across a situation where you need a shell script to pause for a while, you can use the `sleep` command. Simply issue the **sleep** command as follows: **sleep <seconds>**. The shell halts until that many seconds have passed. It then resumes execution of whatever it was doing.

DOING IT CONDITIONALLY: `while` AND `if`

If you want to get sophisticated with the control of your automation, you can turn to conditional statements that can activate certain sections of your script only when certain conditions apply.

To use conditional statements, you need to create a condition for the statement to test. This can be as complicated as you want, but for now, you need to stick to simple things such as equal to.

`while`

The `while` command, with the syntax **while (`<condition>`)**, does things while a certain condition holds.

Although the following example is amusing, consider the situation where you're feeling really lonely and want to get some email. When you execute **/bin/mail**, all it tells you is No mail. A sad day indeed. So, to try to brighten your day, you've written yourself a little script that sends email to a few of your friends every so often, asking them to email you back. Of course you don't want to be such a bozo that it keeps sending them email even after they've replied, so you want it to stop after you've received email, or to only continue while you don't.

If you actually wanted to try this, you might accomplish it by entering a little script such as the following:

```
> set hopeful=(`/bin/mail ¦ grep -cv No`)
> while ($hopeful==0)
? echo "please send me mail" ¦ mail myfriend@somewhere.com
? echo "please send me mail" ¦ mail
➥anotherfriend@elsewhere.com
? sleep 60
? set hopeful=(`/bin/mail ¦ grep -cv No`)
? end
```

This silly little script is making use of grep to count the lines (-c option) which *do not* (-v option) contain a match for No, and assigning the result to the variable named hopeful. Putting the /bin/mail piped into the grep command inside single back-quotes causes the shell to execute those commands and return their output; this output is what gets assigned to the variable hopeful.

Because you don't have mail, and the only response that mail gives when you don't is No mail, there are zero lines which don't contain No initially.

The script uses mail to send out a few pathetic pleas, then goes to sleep for 60 seconds. Afterward, it checks the status of your mailbox again. If you've gotten mail in the interim, mail gives headers instead of the No mail response. In this case, there will be a number other than zero lines which don't match No. (Assuming, of course, that you're not such an unlucky person that your friends reply: "No, we won't reply—go away!") If there are lines which don't contain No, hopeful won't be equal to zero, and the while terminates. If hopeful is still zero, well, your friends' mailboxes will fill up pretty fast...

Using if

The if command works in much the same way as the while command, except it doesn't loop; it simply executes one command based on the condition. The syntax of the if command is as follows: if (*<condition>*) *<command>*.

Using another silly example, if you're irritated by the fact that you have no email and just hate seeing that No mail response, you can use a shell script to do something about it. You might try creating yourself a shell-script file named checkmail with the following contents:

```
#!/bin/csh
set foo=(`/bin/mail | grep -cv No`)
if ($foo == 0) echo "You poor guy"
```

Again, it's going to use /bin/mail to find out whether you have mail; if you don't have mail, well, your computer will commiserate with you.

Summary

Shell scripting can enable you to add functionality and customize your environment. You have the option of doing things as sophisticated as creating small programs, or as simple as automating your daily repetitive tasks. Here's a review of the key points of this lesson:

- Your shell scripts can be stored in files to enable you to execute many commands by simply typing one.

- There are many different shells—yours might work differently than what is presented here, but probably has similar capabilities. If it doesn't, get a better shell!

- The foreach command enables you to repeat a set of commands for each of a number of files

- The while command enables you to repeat a set of commands while a certain condition holds.

- The if command enables you to execute a command—or not execute it—based on a conditional statement.

- The sleep command does nothing for a while—sometimes this is actually useful.

LESSON 15
USER UTILITIES

In this lesson you will learn how to change your password and shell, and to modify other information.

UNIX provides a wealth of utilities to help you control the information that the system stores for your user account. In this lesson, you'll see how to monitor the use of your system through some useful command-line utilities.

CHANGING YOUR PASSWORD: passwd AND yppasswd

One of the most important things you'll need to do in a networked environment is change your password. Passwords generally need to be changed somewhat frequently in order to maintain a secure environment. There are two ways that a password can be changed. If you are in a networked environment you might have to use the yppasswd, which updates your password on all the networked machines. The most obvious way of telling if this is the sort of environment you're working in is if you can log into multiple computers with the same username and password and access the same information. This is a common setup for UNIX computer labs. If your machine is an isolated UNIX computer, just use the passwd command and you will be fine. The two commands operate in an identical manner; it is simply where the updated password is stored that is different.

For example, type the following:

```
>passwd

Changing password for jray
Old password: *****
New password: ******
Retype new password: ******
Password successfully changed
```

The passwords you type are not echoed to the display as you type them. Asterisks were included here to show that typing is taking place. If the password change is successful, UNIX indicates that with a message such as, "Password successfully changed." In some cases, UNIX can keep you from choosing certain passwords if they are too short or based on words in its built-in dictionary file. If your UNIX machine is set up this way and you enter an unacceptable password, the passwd command usually tells you what you need to do to correct it. Choose passwords that mix letters, numbers, and letter cases, and that are not based on common words.

CHANGING YOUR SHELL: chsh

In the beginning of this book, you learned that there are a variety of different shells that you can run. Now you're going to learn how to change them. With the chsh command you can choose one of the shells that is registered for use on the machine. Before you actually change the shell, you might want to see the shells that are available on your computer. You can do this with the chsh -l command, as follows:

```
>chsh -l

/bin/bash
/bin/sh
/bin/ash
/bin/bsh
/bin/tcsh
/bin/csh
/bin/ksh
```

In this example, there are seven different shells that you can choose from. If you wanted to go ahead and change to ksh from your current choice, you would do the following:

```
>chsh

Changing shell for jray.
Password: *****
New shell [/bin/bash]: /bin/ksh
Shell changed.
```

The next time you logged in to your machine, you would be in ksh instead of your previous shell. You probably won't ever need to change your shell, unless the default shell on your system is the Bourne shell (sh). If you want to try other shells, feel free; you can always change back.

GETTING AND CHANGING USER INFORMATION: finger AND chfn

Each user has a few pieces of information about their physical address stored as part of the system password file. This enables other users to quickly find the information necessary to contact them. The command that displays this user data is finger. User information can be stored when the user account is created, but frequently system administrators don't have time to fill this out; so, yours might be incomplete, or even empty. In order to change that, you'll use chfn.

USING finger

Using the finger command is simple. Just use finger <username> to get information about a user who is local to your system. To get information about someone on a remote system, you can try the following: **finger <username>@<remote host>**. Depending on how the remote host is configured, and the type of remote host, it might or might not work.

Look at the following example:

```
>finger jray@poisontooth.com

[poisontooth.com]
Login: jray                          Name: John Ray
Directory: /home/jray                Shell: /bin/bash
On since Sun Nov 29 16:35 (EST) on ttyp0 from 192.168.0.91
    6 hours 47 minutes idle
No mail.
No Plan.
```

This is the finger information returned about a user. As you can see, there isn't much of interest here. This is because there is no personal information set just yet. You can see, however, how long he's been logged into the system, his real name, and his home directory. jray can add personal information to his account profile with chfn.

USING chfn

The chfn command runs an interactive process that enables you to set some personal information for your account. Run **chfn** on a command line without any options, as follows:

```
>chfn
```

```
Changing finger information for jray.
Password: *****
Name [John Ray]: John Ray
Office []: 7879 Rhapsody Drive
Office Phone []: (614) XXX-XXXX
Home Phone []: (614) XXX-XXXX
```

jray can change or set his full name, his office address, and his home and office phone numbers. If you're using chfn and you don't want to set a value, don't—you aren't forced to supply any of this information unless it is the policy of your company. Now that jray has added some information about himself, you can re-run the finger command to see the results. Type the following:

```
>finger jray@poisontooth.com
```

```
[poisontooth.com]
Login: jray                       Name: John Ray
Directory: /home/jray             Shell: /bin/bash
Office: 7879 Rhapsody Drive       Office Phone: (614) XXX-XXXX
Home Phone: (614) XXX-XXXX
On since Sun Nov 29 16:35 (EST) on ttyp0 from 192.168.0.91
    6 hours 48 minutes idle
On since Sun Nov 29 21:47 (EST) on ttyp1 from 192.168.0.211
No mail.
No Plan.
```

That's a bit better! Now the office address and office/home phone numbers are shown correctly. Depending on how you use your system, you might not want to set any of this information. If that's the case, you can feel free to wipe the chfn command from your memory.

MONITORING YOUR SYSTEM: date, uptime, AND who

Now turn your attention to a few commands that you can use to monitor your system. It's nice to be able to see who is logged into your machine, as well as the current status of the computer. Following is a quick look at a trio of commands that will show you information that you might find useful in checking on your computer.

USING date

The date command, as one might guess, returns the current date and time. If you have super-user privileges you can also use date to set the day and time on the computer. Ordinary user accounts do not have this capability. Simply type the following:

```
>date
Mon Nov 30 01:15:17 EST 1998
```

There's nothing to it. You might be wondering why anyone would even take the space to cover such a command. The answer is simple: Without the date command, how do you find out the current day and time information on your computer? If you're using X Windows you might have a clock on your desktop, but outside of the windowing environment, the date command becomes very useful after you have lost all sense of time because you have been staring at your screen for hours on end.

USING uptime

uptime is another simple and useful command. It returns the current time, the number of users logged into the system, how long the system has been running, and the amount of load that the system has been under. Just type **uptime** at the command prompt, as follows:

```
>uptime
1:20am up 2 days, 9:18, 2 users, load average: 1.10,0.90,0.10
```

As you can see from this result, it's 1:20am (yes, it really is!), and the system has been running for two days, nine hours, and 18 minutes since it was last rebooted. There are currently two users logged into the system. The load average is comprised of three values: the first value is the load on the system during the past minute, the second is the load averaged during 10 minutes, and the third, during 15 minutes. These values are rarely more than one or two. If you see a system load average of anything more than five, your computer is *really* busy.

USING who

As you know, UNIX is a multi-user system. This means that there can be several different users logged in at any time. If your system seems slow, you might want to check who is using the computer so you can run over to their desk and yell at them. To see who is logged in, you use the **who** command as follows:

```
>who

jray     ttyp0     Nov 29 16:35 (192.168.0.91)
yort     ttyp1     Nov 29 21:47 (192.168.0.211)
```

There are currently two users logged into the system. who returns the username of each user who is logged in, as well as the name of the controlling terminal, the date and time they logged in, and the IP address from which they are connected.

Remember finger   If you don't recognize one of the users connected to your system, remember the finger command. You can use this command to find out more information about other users on the system.

OTHER COMMAND LINE AND KDE UTILITIES

There are hundreds of other utilities available on your system for monitoring network connections, processing files, and even generating calendars (cal). If you want to explore, you might try listing the files in the /usr/bin and /usr/local/bin directories or reading the man pages for anything that sounds interesting.

The KDE environment provides its own utilities, including a *personal information manager* (*PIM*) called KArm, a floppy formatter called KFloppy, a CD player called KCD, and so on. There is simply no way a single reference book can touch on all these topics completely. Your best bet is to look through the file system and research the commands that look interesting. The extensive man page collection available for command-line utilities provides excellent reference information. KDE also provides comprehensive online help, which makes life pretty easy.

SUMMARY

UNIX has tons of built-in utilities. In this lesson, you learned about several of the programs which modify information related to your account profile, as well as a few utilities to monitor the state of your computer and who is currently using it. Following is a look at what else was discussed in this lesson:

- **passwd/yppasswd**—The passwd command changes your account password. If you're in an environment with networked UNIX computers, you might have to use the yppasswd command instead.

- **chsh**—Use the change shell command to change your current shell. If you don't know for sure which shell you want to switch to, you can use chsh -l to list the available shells on your system.

- **finger**—This command looks up personal information about an account on your computer, or on a remote computer. finger is sometimes disabled for security reasons, so you might not be able to use finger to get the results you expect.

- **chfn**—Change finger information using this command. With this you can change your full name, as well as the office address and office/home phone numbers in your account profile.

- **date**—Simply enough, date displays the current day and time on your computer.

- **uptime**—The uptime command provides a summary of information about the state of your operating system, including the length of time it has been online, the number of users logged in, and the average load on your system for the past 15 minutes.

- **who**—who enables you to see all the users who are logged in to your computer, the date that they connected, and from what network address they are connected. If your machine seems slow, you might want to use who to find out where all the processor time is going.

- **Other utilities**—There are far too many utilities on the system to cover them all in this book. Luckily, the man pages provide extensive documentation for most programs on the system. In addition, KDE has its own comprehensive documentation system.

Lesson 16

Modifying the User Environment

In this lesson you'll learn about the tools you need to use to modify your environment and the way that some commands work for you.

There is a vast number of programs that all work together to create the UNIX user experience. It's because of this that you'll need to learn to use the tools from this section in conjunction with the documentation for your programs to make the modifications you desire.

 Shell Assumption This lesson is going to assume that you're using csh or tcsh as your shell. If you are using a different shell, some of the syntax needs to be changed, but the ideas remain the same.

Aliases

One of the most useful features that shells provide to the user is the capability to create command aliases. *Aliases* are, quite simply, aliases. If, for example, you're a long-time DOS user, you might find yourself typing del instead of rm to delete files. Want to change this? Just set an alias with the alias command. The syntax is as follows: **alias <newname> <command to run>**. If you actually want to make that alias for del, type the following: **alias del rm**. After setting this alias, any time you type del, it executes the command rm.

More useful than simply renaming commands, you can use the alias command to create *meta* commands that enforce certain options. For example, it's always a good idea to force rm to be in interactive mode (rm -i). To do this with an alias, you can type the following: **alias rm 'rm -i'**. (Note the direction of the single quotes.) Now, whenever you type rm it actually executes rm -i instead.

If you want to get really sophisticated with aliases, you can even build little multi-command scripts inside aliases. For example, consider the situation where you want to access two different news servers from your account. In this case, perhaps it's a public server for regular Usenet News newsgroups, and a corporate server for internal news. The trn and rn commands only understand one news server at a time, and worse, save the "What I have read" information in a file with a fixed name. What to do? Use the alias command to automate things for you. The following two aliases will solve your problem:

```
> alias readcorporate 'setenv NNTPSERVER
➡server.big.company.com;\
                        cp ~/.corp-newsrc ~/.newsrc;\
                        trn;
                        cp ~/.newsrc ~/.corp-newsrc'
> alias readpublic    'setenv NNTPSERVER
➡public.newsstand.com;\
                        cp ~/.public-newsrc ~/.newsrc;\
                        trn;
                        cp ~/.newsrc ~/.public-newsrc'
```

What do they do? Following is an explanation:

- The first line of each sets an environment variable which tells trn where to look to get its news. There is more on this in the next section.

- The second line of each copies a setting file to the file .newsrc in your home directory. The trn command uses the file .newsrc to keep track of what news you've read and what is new news. If you're using two different servers with two different sets of newsgroups, you unfortunately can't use the same .newsrc file, so you'll keep two of them around and let alias copy the correct one for you when you need it.

- The third line is self-explanatory. The trn command reads Usenet newsgroups. There is a little more on this in Lesson 18, "Accessing the Network Resources."

- The fourth line might be a bit of a mystery at first, but it's really quite simple as well. Because the trn command updates the .newsrc file with information on what you've just read, you want to preserve the file for the next time you read news; so, you copy it back to its holding location.

Now all you have to do to read your news from your corporate news server server.big.company.com is type **readcorporate**, and to read your public Usenet newsgroups you just type **readpublic**.

ENVIRONMENT VARIABLES

As mentioned much earlier in this book, most of the software you use, and the interface you work in when using UNIX, is configured with seemingly cryptic text files. Other pieces of software are configured by special shell variables called *Environment Variables*. (Remember shell variables from Lesson 14, "Basic Shell Scripting.")

Environment Variables are used by programs to pick up specific pieces of information that are needed to run. For example, you might run across programs that want an environment variable that contains the path to their help-file information. Others use Environment Variables to contain custom settings for things such as window size or placement preferences. In the preceding aliases section, you might have noticed a program that wanted an Environment Variable set to tell it what Internet host to contact.

Environment variables aren't set using quite the same syntax as regular shell variables, so instead of using set *<variablename>=<value>*, use the following syntax:

setenv <variablename> <value>.

Consider the situation where you have a program that says to set the Environment Variable HELPFILE_LOC to the directory containing its help information. Unless this variable is set, it can't find the information it needs and it won't work properly. If you've found that the help file is located in the directory /usr/local/helpstuff, you can set the variable you need by using the following command:

```
> setenv HELPFILE_LOC /usr/local/helpstuff
```

The number of programs that use Environment Variables for configuration information is quite large, but the format is always the same. All you need to do is find out what variable needs to be set, and then set it to the correct value.

 Using printenv If you want to see the Environment Variables that are already set in your shell, you can use the printenv command.

If you're running X Windows and trying to display on a different machine than the one on which you're running the client, you might have to set the DISPLAY variable as follows: **setenv DISPLAY <machinename>:0.0**.

If you've run a program and it exits with a complaint such as ld.so not found, you might have to set the LD_LIBRARY_PATH with a command such as **setenv LD_LIBRARY_PATH /usr/local/lib**.

The possibilities really are endless—thankfully, making the settings is a relatively painless process. Just remember that the settings you make in one shell do not affect other shells. You can have the same Environment Variable set to different values in different shells you're running simultaneously if you need to access more than one configuration at a time.

PATHS

Another special shell variable is the *path variable*. It tells the shell where to look for programs that you want to execute. Remember how long the find command took to find things for you (refer to Lesson 5, "Finding Files")? Because you don't want it to take that long every time you try to execute a program, you don't want the system to have to search through everything on your machine to find a program. Instead, the shell keeps a short list of where to look for programs and it only searches these locations.

Shells and Executable Files Technically, it doesn't even search these locations when you try to execute a program. The shell actually keeps a catalog of all the executable files found in these locations. If a new executable appears in one of these locations while you're logged in, your shells won't know about it until you execute the `rehash` command, which asks the shell to go back and rebuild the catalog.

You might notice that if you have a copy of a program in your current directory, in some cases typing the filename results in a `command not found` error. This is because it's common for the path variable to lack the current directory. You can either execute programs in the current directory by typing `./<programname>` or by adding the current directory to your path.

Working with Paths The current directory is usually left out of the path because including it is a bit of a security risk. If the current directory is in your path, you can potentially be fooled into executing arbitrary programs by naming them as common UNIX commands and sneaking them into your directories. If you want to put the current directory in your path, always put it at the end of the path. That way normal UNIX commands will be found before any Trojan horses that might have made their way into your system.

If you want to see what your current path is, you can do so by using `echo $path`. If it's missing some paths you need, for instance the current directory and /usr/local/bin, you can add these by using the following command:

```
set path=($path /usr/local/bin .)
```

USER DEFAULTS: THE DOT FILES

Your account configures certain features for you automatically when you log in and when you start shells. Programs other than the shell also occasionally use *dot files* to hold configuration information. Dot files are, literally, files with names starting with the . character, and you're likely to find an abundance already populating your home directory. Some common files follow:

- **.login and .logout**—As you might guess, files which are executed when you log in, and when you log out, respectively. If you look in these files you will find that they are shell scripts which use commands with which you are already familiar. The .login shell script is typically used for things such as swapping in various sets of configuration files if you want to set up multiple different environments for yourself, and for doing other things that need to be handled automatically at login. The .logout script is used much less frequently, but it can contain useful things that you need to do at logout time. What sort of use can you make of the .login and .logout files? How about adding commands which echo the date and time information into a file whenever you log in and log out. If you've ever had to fill out a timesheet, you'll find that one appealing.

- **.cshrc or .profile**—Shell scripts that are executed when you open a shell. Shells have their own scripts which execute at startup. Check with your shell's documentation on this. Again, you are familiar with the syntax. In this file, you can include commands that do things such as add custom paths to your environment, set Environment Variables, and set up any aliases you might be interested in.

- **.plan**—A file that contains information that your system sends back to anyone who fingers you. Users typically use their .plan file to contain contact information, favorite quotes, and anecdotes that they consider amusing. Put things in your plan that you want people to see when they try to look you up from remote. After you've put something in your .plan file, give the finger command a try and see how your new information looks.

- **.X11defaults or .Xdefaults**—This file contains settings that are used by the server resource database. The syntax of this file was covered briefly in Lesson 3, "The Graphical User Interface." In general, you won't need to modify this file, but it is here that you can configure many options regarding how the X server treats various programs and how various X11 programs work. If you choose to poke around in it, be sure to make a backup copy first, in case you have to put it back. After you have made a backup, though, don't be afraid to make modifications. The syntax is straightforward, and if you've survived this far, you can probably figure out how to make most of the modifications that you might want to try.

You'll undoubtedly find that you have other dot files in your directories as well. Don't be afraid to look in them. You'll find most to be more readable than you might think. Although it might be a bit intimidating at first, a large part of making UNIX work for you is customizing your environment by modifying these files. Make backups first, but don't be afraid to experiment—it's half the joy of using UNIX!

FIXING BROKEN TERMINALS: stty

On occasion, you might find yourself in a command-line window that seems to have gone slightly nuts. The Delete key produces ^?, the Backspace key makes a ^H, and Ctrl+c shows ^C. If this happens to you, you need to reset the terminal parameters for erase and interrupt. To do this, enter the two following commands:

```
> stty erase Delete
> stty intr Ctrl+c
```

Using stty   To make your life easier, some versions of stty now support assignment by using the carat notation for the control characters. Instead of actually having to type **Ctrl+c** in the preceding stty intr example, you might be able to type **stty intr ^C**.

You can also use **stty erase Backspace** if your keyboard layout makes Backspace more convenient than Delete. If your terminal has gone completely insane and the Return key no longer seems to be working correctly, you can try using the following command: **stty sane Ctrl+j**. This command attempts to reset the terminal to its default settings, but it isn't guaranteed to work.

CHANGING KDE'S APPEARANCE

Like most desktop environments, KDE includes the capability to customize your desktop environment just as you do under Windows or MacOS. You can set the background, screensaver, fonts, and other attributes of the windowing environment. The changes you make are not system-wide changes; they affect only your personal settings, so feel free to customize to your heart's content! A sample of the different settings that you can customize is shown in Figure 16.1.

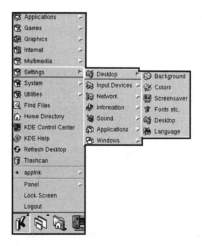

FIGURE 16.1   KDE offers a wide selection of custom configuration options.

Use the following steps to change KDE's appearance:

1. Click the main **K** toolbar menu item.

2. Choose the **Settings** item from the menu.

3. Select the property you want to change (**Desktop**, **Sound**, and so on).

4. Choose any appropriate sub-property from the category you've chosen. For example, the **Desktop** enables you to change colors, background, and fonts, among others.

5. Make the changes you want, and then click the **Apply** or **OK** button to set them.

SUMMARY

In this lesson, you were introduced to the idea of modifying your environment settings by the use of aliases, Environment Variables, and configuration files. Making these modifications is what enables you to make the environment you work in your own. Following is a review of what was covered in this lesson:

- Environment Variables are frequently used for specifying single configuration options to a program, such as providing a pointer to a directory that the program needs.

- The path variable keeps track of where the system searches for commands when you type them. If a command exists on the system, but the path to the command is not in your path variable, it will not be found when you type the command name.

- Aliases are a very powerful feature of UNIX shells. They enable you to rename commands, or cause commands to always use certain options when you issue them.

- Dot files are everywhere. Many programs use text files containing configuration information for control purposes. These files almost universally have filenames which start with a . character. They are the place to look for automating settings to your shell, and for configuring options for the windowing system.

- The stty command can rescue your terminal session if something has caused it to begin behaving oddly.

Don't be afraid to experiment. You've just made it through a lesson on modifying your user environment. Now go out and do it!

LESSON 17
PRINTING

In this lesson you'll learn how you can print requests (or jobs) to a printer on your network.

As you might be coming to expect, UNIX abstracts the notion of the physical location of the printer, so both local (directly-connected) and remote printers are accessed in the same fashion.

An early divergence in the evolution of UNIX caused there to be two different UNIX printing methodologies: the *lp* system and the *lpd* system. lpd was created on the *Berkeley Standard Distribution (BSD)* UNIX source base, and lp was created on the *AT&T System V* source base. Unfortunately for the user, these systems are just different enough to make life confusing. From a system administrator's point of view, lp seems to have been created specifically to make life more difficult. Because of this you will find many UNIX machines that are running OS versions based on System V, that have had lp replaced with the BSD lpd system.

SENDING A PRINT JOB: `lpr` OR `lp`

In UNIX, many people can be printing at a single time. Because of this, when you send a print request to a printer it is assigned a job number. If you need to cancel your print job, this number is used to remove the job from the print queue. Only the root user or the person who owns a print job can remove it from the queue.

Postscript vs. Non-Postscript The assumption is made throughout this lesson that you are printing to a Postscript printer. It is possible, however, that your system might be configured to interpret Postscript using a rasterizer, and to print to a non-Postscript printer.

If you're lucky enough to have the `lpd` system available on your machine, you can use the `lpr` suite of programs. If you're on a machine that uses `lp`, watch for the sections pointing out `lp` differences.

The `lpr` (*line printer*) command is the primary method for sending data to the printer. `lpr` essentially dumps data directly to the printer you specify. To use `lpr`, follow these steps:

1. Determine the name of the printer you want to use. This was probably set by your system administrator.

2. Choose the file you want to print. For the moment, only chose a text file. You'll get to see a few other formats shortly.

3. Send the print job by using the following command: **lpr -P<printer name> <filename> <filename>** .... If there is only one printer configured on your computer, chances are you can simply type **lpr <filename> <filename>** ....

> **Be Careful...** There's no space between that -P and the printer name.

For example, type the following:

```
>lpr -Phod samplefile.txt
```

The result of this command is that the file samplefile.txt is sent to the printer named hod. Depending on the load of the printer, the print job will probably be processed shortly.

> **Printing More than One Copy** If you need to print multiple copies of a document, you don't need to send separate print jobs. Instead, you can specify the number of copies as an option to the `lpr` command. Simply follow **lpr** with -#<number of copies> to print that many copies of each file in the job.

There are a few file formats and special print cases that might require special attention from the print command. This special attention comes in the form of *filters* that are applied to the file and convert the information into a format that your printer can handle. Following are some filters:

- **.ps**   Postscript files. Postscript files will be handled automatically by the lpr command. You can print them as you print a plain text file.

- **.dvi**   Tex files. Files from tex contain special page layout instructions. You can use the -d option with lpr in order to print these files correctly.

- **.tr**   Troff files. This is the standard file format for man pages. If you want to print out a man page you can use the -t option.

- **Text files with really long lines**   If you are having problems printing text files because lines are running off the end of the page, you can have the files reformatted on-the-fly so that they fit. To do this, use -p with lpr.

System Quirks   It's not unusual for a system to be configured without most of the previously mentioned filters installed. You can expect that a conscientious system administrator will have configured your system to handle postscript and plain text properly, but you might find that many have left handling the remainder up to you. In this case you'll have to find and use the appropriate software to process your data files into postscript or plain text, and then send these processed files to the lpr command.

Using lp and lpr   The lp command works much like the lpr command, but with enough differences to make it annoying to the user familiar with lpr.

Instead of using a -P option to specify the printer, you use a -d option.

Use -n<*number of copies*> instead of -#<*number of copies*>.

When you send a job to the printer with lp, it gives you a message such as the following: request id is <*uniquename*>-#. Remember this <*uniquename*>-# combination because that's what you'll need to know to remove the job if you decide you don't want it to print after all.

The lp system is supposed to make your life easier by handling detection of file types and appropriate conversions automatically. Instead of specific options for specific types of files, however, every type of printer and every installation can have different options available. Hopefully, you will never need to know these installation-specific options, but if you do, check your local documentation to find out what your system can do.

CHECKING THE STATUS OF A PRINT JOB: lpq

After you've sent a job to the printer, chances are you'll want to be able to check to see if it is done printing   especially if it is a network printer located on another floor in your building or in another building altogether! To check the status of a job, you'll want to look at the queue for the printer to which you submitted the job. You do this with the **lpq -P<*printer name*>** command. Once again, if there is only a single printer on your system, you can probably just issue lpq by itself.

For example, type the following:

```
>lpq -Phod
```

Rank	Owner	Job	Files	Total Size
1st	agroves	27	test.txt	19 bytes
2nd	jray	28	samplefile.txt	10021 bytes

This example shows that there are currently two different jobs in the printer queue for hod. One is owned by agroves, and the user jray owns the second. Each job is ranked; this shows the order in which it will print. The names of the files being printed are also shown, as are the size and job ID number.

 Status Check   Instead of lpq, the lp system uses lpstat. The easiest way to find out everything about your lp printing system is to use the following command: **lpstat -t**. This lists all the printers that are available on your system, and all the jobs on the listed printers.

CANCELING A PRINT JOB: lprm

At times you might find that you've sent a print request to the printer when you didn't actually mean to   perhaps you sent a 3,000 page ency-clopedia file instead of the three page report that you intended to send. Whatever the case, there is a command that enables you to remove items from the printer queue: lprm.

If you need to use lprm, follow these steps:

1. Use the lpq command to find the Job ID number that you want to remove.

2. Invoke lprm with the following syntax: **lprm -P<printer name> <job ID>**.

For example, if you wanted to remove job #28 from the queue in the last example (assuming that you're the jray user), you'd type the following:

```
>lprm -Phod 28
```

To verify the results, you can use lpq to check the queue again:

```
>lpq -Phod
```

Rank	Owner	Job	Files	Total Size
1st	agroves	27	test.txt	19 bytes

Job #28 is no longer in the queue, and will not be printed. Don't worry if you happen to accidentally enter someone else's print job ID   you can only cancel your own jobs.

If you want to remove all the pending print jobs that you have sent, you can use the - character in place of the job ID. This cancels anything that you've sent to the printer.

 Canceling a Print Job   The lp system uses the command cancel instead of lprm. To cancel a printer job, use the lpstat -t command to list the jobs, pick the job ID, and then issue the cancel command as follows: cancel *<jobid>*. Because lp keeps track of print job IDs with unique names rather than just numbers, there is no need for you to specify from which printer you want to remove the job.

PRETTY PRINTING: ENSCRIPT

If you want to do some fancy printing, you can use the enscript command to convert your text files into postscript and add some flashy features. (This might not be installed on all systems—ask your system administrator to install this if you need it and can't find it.) For instance, if you want to print two pages of text on a single side of paper, enscript can format your document correctly. It can also print banner information with each page to help you identify what file has been printed and what page number you are looking at.

To use enscript in its most basic form, do the following:

1. Choose your printer.

2. Choose the file that you want to print.

3. Run enscript as follows: **enscript -d** *<printer name>* *<filename>* *<filename>* **....**

For example, to use enscript to print the file samplefile.txt, you type the following:

```
>enscript -d hod samplefile.txt

[ 1 pages * 1 copy ] sent to printer
```

Unlike `lpr`, `enscript` gives a bit of feedback on what is happening. Here it tells the user that it has sent one page to the printer, and has requested the default number of copies: one. The output of this command, in its basic form, is very similar to that of `lpr`. It simply dumps the file to the printer. The difference, however, lies in the command-line options that you can add to `enscript` to change the appearance of your printout. Following are some of the options you can use:

- **Page range**—Use the option `-a <start page>-<end page>` to print a range of pages, rather than everything.

- **Pretty print source-code**—If you're a programmer, `enscript` can print your source in an attractive format with highlights if you use the `-E` command-line switch.

- **Fancy header**—If you want to easily identify the file and page number that the text on a page belongs to, you can ask enscript to print a *fancy header* using `-G`.

- **Landscape mode**—Rather than printing across the short dimension of your page, the `-r` option rotates the page 90 degrees and prints in landscape mode.

- **Multiple columns**—To print two pages of text per printed page, use the `-2` option. You'll probably also want to use the `-r` Landscape mode switch so that everything fits appropriately.

- **Highlight bars**—If you're reading source code or spreadsheet-type data, you might find it difficult to follow a line across a page. Use the `-H` option to print light gray highlight bars across the page.

- **Multiple copies**—Using a slightly different syntax than `lpr`, `enscript` can print multiple copies of a job using the `-n <number of copies>` option.

Although I'm sure that you don't need to be reminded at this point, be sure to check the man pages for more information on `enscript`. There are many more options that you can use to further customize the appearance of your printouts.

SUMMARY

In this lesson, you learned the commands you need to print from the command line. If you're using an application in the KDE environment, it is actually using the same commands you've seen here to send information to the printer. The suite of `lpr`, `lpq`, and `lprm` commands make up the basis for printing from UNIX and most UNIX computers. `enscript` is the icing on the cake. Here's a review of some of the highlights of this lesson:

- **`lpr` and `lp`**—The `lpr` and `lp` commands are used to send a file to the printer. If the file is of a type other than plain text, it can be processed by a filter to correctly format the information for your printer.

- **`lpq` and `lpstat`**—When a print request is sent to the printer, either from `lpr` or `enscript`, it is added to the printer queue. Use the `lpq` or `lpstat -t` program to display all pending printer transactions, their corresponding job IDs, and their owners.

- **`lprm` and `cancel`**—If you want to remove a job from the print queue, `lprm` or `cancel` will do the trick.

- **`enscript`**—`enscript` is a useful utility for doing fancy printing on your printer. It allows multiple pages of text per printer page, pretty graphic headers, and a variety of other goodies.

LESSON 18

ACCESSING THE
NETWORK
RESOURCES

In this lesson you will learn about another of the strengths of UNIX, network connectivity.

You're now almost finished with your whirlwind tour of the UNIX operating system, but you are nowhere near finished exploring and learning about the capabilities that UNIX puts at your fingertips.

UNIX excels at networking. As mentioned when discussing UNIX's file system design, with the proper configuration you could spread UNIX machines around the globe and at each one at which you logged in your user environment, files and programs would all appear—just as they do at home.

With the same ease with which your home environment can distribute itself to scattered machines to work for you, so can you distribute your workload to those same machines from your home machine. This lesson will provide you with a survey of some of the programs that allow this distribution of workload.

telnet

telnet is a simple terminal program. In its primary use, it enables you to open a login session on a remote machine. To use the telnet command, issue the command as follows: **telnet <remote machine>**, where <remote machine> is either an IP address or a hostname. You will be prompted with a login and password prompt just as if you were sitting at the console of the remote machine.

TELNET PARTICULARS It's not unusual to run into situations where Backspace and Delete don't work properly at the `telnet` login and password prompt. Don't be alarmed; this is simply an indication that the remote machine doesn't yet know what sort of terminal you're using. If the problem persists into the login session, see the section on `stty` in Lesson 16, "Modifying the User Environment."

rlogin

The `rlogin` command is very similar to the `telnet` command, except that it carries some user information along with the attempt to connect. If your account is good on several machines, they might be set up to enable you to connect between them without having to log in to each one. Try the `rlogin` command as follows: **`rlogin <remote machine>`**. If you're lucky, you'll end up in a shell on the remote machine. If you're not, you'll be presented with a login prompt; from there, `rlogin` functions identically to `telnet`.

slogin

The `slogin` command is a remote terminal program that offers strong encryption of the data stream. You are strongly encouraged to use this command if your machines have the secure-shell server running. Both the `rlogin` and `telnet` commands send your login and password information, as well as anything else you type, over the network in plain text. A malicious user with a small amount of easily available *cracker* software can *sniff* this information and compromise your account. (Please don't call them *hackers*. Hackers are quick and dirty, and are often brilliant programmers. They don't break into things—crackers do.)

To find out whether the secure shell server is running, and to set up the `slogin` command (which needs quite a bit of configuration before you can use it), you are advised to contact your system administrator. He or she will be more than happy to tell you about the `slogin` command or any alternatives, and to help you increase system security.

rn/trn

The rn and trn commands read Usenet newsgroups. Although they have retreated slightly into the background because of the World Wide Web, Usenet newsgroups were once considered to be the collective memory of the Net. Even though the Web has eclipsed newsgroups in terms of visibility, the fact that newsgroups function as topic-oriented *chat rooms* and provide almost real-time interaction makes them still a useful source of help and information. You can use the rn or trn command to access information that ranges from the technical, to the idiotic, to the sublime. The rn and trn commands are executed simply by name, and internally take both single-key commands and multi-character commands followed by **Return**. The primary commands you need to know when you are in rn or trn are as follows:

- **The commands for listing newsgroups**—l *<topic>***Return** lists all newsgroups that contain that topic. For your topics, keep small parts of words—such as *comp* for *computer topics*—until you become familiar with the newsgroup naming conventions.

- **The command for going to a newsgroup**—Type g **<newsgroup name>Return**, and then follow the instructions.

- **The command for help**—h (no **Return**) brings up rather copious context-sensitive help at almost any point in the program.

The trn command is a slightly more sophisticated version of rn, offering article selection by subject thread; you will probably prefer it if it's available. Either version can be highly configured with command-line switches and configuration files.

ftp

The ftp command provides you with a way to retrieve files from remote machines that aren't set up to share file systems with yours. If your machine is running an ftp-server, you might be able to use it to provide your files to the rest of the world as well. Contact your system administrator about this.

To use the ftp command, simply enter the command as follows: **ftp <ftp server>**, where the ftp-server is the IP address or hostname of a remote machine running an ftp-server. If you've connected properly, you'll get a prompt for a username and password.

Some ftp-servers enable you to connect without an account on the system. For these, use the username *anonymous* and give your email address as the password.

Once connected to an ftp-site, you can cd and ls your way around. Using the command **get <filename>** enables you to retrieve a file and **put <filename>** enables you to send one from your directory to the remote system.

CORRUPTING YOUR DATA   Some ftp-servers corrupt data unless you issue the command binary after you are connected. They're actually trying to fix the difference between the way that UNIX and PC-type machines handle carriage-returns in files, but they just end up screwing things up when talking to another UNIX machine. If you end up with corrupted files after you've downloaded them, try again, but issue the binary command before the get command.

Web Browsers: Netscape and Lynx

The following sections discuss the Netscape and Lynx Web browsers.

Netscape

Netscape is the GUI-based Web browser that is available on the largest number of UNIX platforms. It functions in much the same way as the Macintosh or PC versions that you might already be familiar with—point, click, and repeat as necessary. If it's available on your system, you can most likely start Netscape by simply typing **netscape** in any X Windows terminal.

Lynx

Lynx is a text-based Web-browser, for those times when you're stuck in a text window. Start it with this command: **lynx <URL>**. You get a textual representation of the page, at which the URL points. Lynx is a surprisingly full-featured browser for what you might think is an extremely limited market. The market is actually a bit bigger than you might think. Lynx starts and loads pages much faster than graphic-based browsers. This makes it a convenient alternative if you need to check a Web page quickly and don't need either the graphics or the wait.

Email

Of all the network tools you'll make use of from your UNIX account, email is likely to be the most frequently used. Email enables you to communicate with your friends and colleagues, exchange files, and contact people all over the planet. As is fitting to its position of most-used tool, email also has the widest range of software available. Most versions of UNIX come with at least two different programs for accessing email, and frequently have a handful of others that have been installed over time. Although they are only a small sampling of the programs available, the following programs are commonly used for accessing and working with email:

- **Mail**—Found on almost all UNIX systems, Mail is a command-line driven mail reading system. It's a fairly simple program without many customization features, but it's fast and convenient to use if you don't need fancy mail filters or a menu-driven interface.

- **mail**—Also found on almost all UNIX systems, mail is not something you want to use for reading mail unless you absolutely must. You will usually find that the major use for mail is using it in shell scripts, as has been demonstrated in several places in this book.

- **pine and elm**—Not standard on most commercial UNIX flavors, pine and elm are both full-screen mail reading programs with simple-to-use and intuitive menus and configuration options. The pine program is somewhat more powerful than elm, but both are good mail readers for users who want convenience in a text-based email reader.

- **mh**—The Mail Handler. The mh suite of programs must be close to the least, if not the least, intuitive mail reading package available. It is also the most powerful by far. The mh philosophy is very similar to the UNIX philosophy—break the job at hand down into the smallest building blocks possible, make each of these programs, and enable the user to put them together to make any custom configuration desired. Only choose mh as your mail reader when you've become comfortable doing a bit of shell script programming because you have to construct custom aliases and scripts before mh shows you its true power.

- **procmail**—The Mail Processor. The procmail program is designed to do sophisticated automatic processing of your email as it is received. If you want to add automatic processing of your email to your account, you might want to check whether procmail is available on your system.

- **Graphical email interfaces**—Many desktop environments provide graphical email readers. For the user interested in the ultimate in point-and-click convenience, look to your desktop environment software. Netscape additionally provides an email client on UNIX platforms, but it is only a popmail client and cannot read from your UNIX mail spool unless your machine is also running a POP3 server. An example of the KDE email client (appropriately named *Mail client*) is shown in Figure 18.1.

FIGURE **18.1**   KDE provides several graphic network clients, including an email client.

The .forward File

If you want email that comes to your account to automatically send itself somewhere else, you can make use of the .forward file. Not only can the .forward file be used to forward your email to another email address, but it can also be used to forward your email into programs if you want to use software to process your email.

The format of the .forward file is simple:

- To forward your email to another email address, create a file named .forward in your home directory. Into this file, put a single line containing the address to which you want your mail forwarded. Execute the command **chmod 644 ~/.forward** to set the permissions properly (some flavors of UNIX are particular about this), and you're done. All email coming to your account is forwarded to the new address.

- To forward your email into a program for automatic processing, create the .forward file in your home directory. In the .forward file, put a single line containing the pipe character ¦ followed by the path to the program that you want to use. Run chmod on the file as with forwarding your email to another account, and you're done. Incoming email is then piped into whatever command you put in the .forward file.

Summary

In this lesson, you were introduced to a sampling of tools that enable you to make use of the network resources around you—and around the world. As you explore UNIX you'll find that this was really only a small sampling, and that there are new tools for you to use appearing constantly. Some will be replacements or upgrades for the commands outlined here, and others will be completely new. Don't be afraid to try them out. Here's a quick review of this lesson's key points:

- The telnet command can connect you to remote machines. If you have different accounts on different machines, you'll probably find yourself using it frequently.

- The rlogin command also connects you to remote machines, but is more useful than telnet if the machines you work on are configured to allow you to rlogin between them without giving a username or password.

- The slogin command provides security for remote connections. If you have it, use it. With people breaking into UNIX machines daily, the network is becoming a very scary place. Using the secure connection provided by slogin protects your network traffic from prying eyes.

- The trn and rn commands read Usenet newsgroups. Newsgroups can be a lot of fun and useful in finding information, but they can also be a big drain on your time.

- The ftp command connects you with ftp servers and enables you to transfer files around the world.

- Netscape is available for many UNIX platforms. Lynx is a fast text-based Web browser. Both are useful for accessing World Wide Web resources.

- You're likely to have a wide choice of options for accessing email. Check with other users of your system to find out what's available and what local configuration information you need.

LESSON 19

PERMISSIONS

In this lesson you will learn what permissions are, and how to change them.

UNIX file permissions might be something that you never have to deal with, but if you want to share files with other users on your system, chances are you need to know a little bit about the concept.

OWNERS, GROUPS, AND PERMISSIONS

The owner of a file is exactly what it sounds like—the person who owns the file. Each file has information stored with it that identifies the account that owns it. Files can be given to other users by changing the owner information to match their username. In general, the person who creates a file is the person who owns it.

Each file on the UNIX system also has a secondary piece of information stored that records the *group* ownership of the file. Groups are collections of users. By allowing a group to share ownership of files, many people can work together on a project and have their changes immediately available to other members of the group. Creation of groups is a system administration task, so if you need a group created for a project, talk to your system administrator.

Permissions control what actions a user can perform on a file or directory. There are three basic actions, which are pretty much self-explanatory: read, write, and execute. *Read* permissions control whether someone can view a file. *Write* allows or disallows changes to be made to a file. Lastly, *execute* permissions control whether a file can be run, or *executed*. In the case of a directory, these change a bit. If a directory has execute permissions turned off, you cannot cd into the directory, view its contents, or write to it. It is effectively turned off. If read permissions are turned off, you can still create files in the directory and read them, but you cannot get a listing of what is in the directory. Lastly, if the write permission for a directory is turned off, you can view a listing of the contents and read files, but you cannot create any new files.

When permissions are applied to a file or folder, they are applied at three distinct levels: owner, group, and world. The *owner* permissions simply control what permissions the file owner has. *Group* permissions determine what actions can be performed by members of the same group to which the file belongs. Your system administrator can create new groups or add you to be a member of a group. You can think of *world* permissions as being permissions for a huge group that encompasses all the users on your computer. If there is any sort of guest access to your computer, you can assume that any active world permissions apply to anyone who can access your computer.

CHECKING THE OWNER, GROUP, AND ASSOCIATED PERMISSIONS: `ls -1`

You've already used the `ls` command extensively, but you probably haven't been paying too much attention to the extended information it can return. If you run `ls -1` to list your directories, you can see the owner, group, and associated permissions for any file.

For example, type the following:

```
>ls -1

-rw-r--r-- 1 jray  jray     2024 Oct 26 20:39 kiwi.tar
-rw------- 1 jray  test  1463882 Jul  2 11:33 magical-beans.gz
drwxrwxr-x 5 jray  test     1024 Nov  5 12:25 kyitn
...
```

Listing Owners and Groups   Some versions of `ls` won't show you the owner and group simultaneously with this command. Usually, they list group and owner if you add the `-g` option, as in `ls -1g`.

The information you're interested in here is in the first, third, and fourth columns:

- The first column identifies the owner, group, and world permissions that are active for a file or directory. The first character is a *d* if the filetype is a directory. Normally this is a - for a normal file. The remainder of the characters, as you might guess, stand for *read*, *write*, and *execute* (*x*). The first three characters (following the initial - or *d* character) are the active owner permissions, the second three characters are the group permissions, and the last three are world permissions.

- The third column is the file owner.

- The fourth column is the group owner.

In this example, the kiwi.tar file has read/write permissions for the owner, and read permissions active for the group and world. The owner of the file is jray and the group that the file belongs to is jray. The second file, magical-beans.gz, only has read/write permissions for the owner, (jray). The group that magical-beans.gz belongs to is test; the group test has no permissions to operate on the file. The last "file," kyitn, is actually a directory. The owner of kyitn is jray and the corresponding group is test. The owner and group both have full read, write, and execute permissions for this directory, whereas the world has only read and execute.

CHANGING PERMISSIONS: chmod

Now that you know what permissions are, you probably want to know how to change them. This is accomplished with the chmod command. There are two modes of operation that you can use with chmod: a quick-and-dirty mode, and a more user-friendly method of setting permissions.

The symbolic user-friendly mode uses easy-to-remember commands to set or unset permissions. To use this, do the following:

1. Pick a *permission level*. If you want to set permissions for the owner, the level is *u*. If you want to change permissions for the group, it is *g*. For world permissions, choose *o*. Lastly, if you want to affect all the levels of permissions (owner, group, and world), use *a*.

2. Choose an *operation*. Decide whether you want to set (turn on) or unset (turn off) a particular level of permission. If you want to set a permission, the operation is +; if you want to unset a permission, it is -.

3. Choose the *permission* itself. If you want to operate on the read permission, choose *r*, for write choose *w*, and for execute choose *x*.

4. Issue the chmod command in this manner: **chmod <*permission level*><*operation*><*permission*> <*filename*> <*filename*> ....**

For example, if you want to activate group write permissions for the "magical-beans.gz" file shown earlier, type the following:

```
-rw------- 1 jray   test 1463882 Jul  2 11:33 magical-beans.gz
>chmod g+w magical-beans.gz
```

To see if this worked, you can run **ls -l** on the filename as follows:

```
>ls -l magical-beans.gz
```

```
-rw--w---- 1 jray   test 1463882 Jul  2 11:33 magical-beans.gz
```

Sure enough, write permissions are now active for the test group members.

Because of its symbolic nature, this method for adjusting file permissions might be easy for some; however, there is another syntax that you might find faster and easier. This deals with setting the actual *bit mask* that controls a file's permissions. Turning on one of three binary bits can represent each level of permissions. The first of these bits (from left to right) controls read, the second controls write, and the third toggles execute.

Look at it this way:

```
100 - Read permission - The decimal equivalent of
➥this binary value is 4.
010 - Write permission - The decimal value for write is 2.
001 - Execute permission - The decimal representation is 1.
```

Using this technique, you can easily set multiple permissions at once. For example, it's easy to see that 110 is the combination of the read and write permissions. The decimal value of this binary string is 6 (4+2). To use this method of setting a file's permissions, you set permissions for owner, group, and world simultaneously—with three digits. Each of these digits is the sum of the permissions that you want to set. The first digit is the owner, the second is the group, and the third is world.

For example, suppose that you want to set the owner to have full permissions, and the group and world to have read and execute permissions. Full permissions are achieved by adding all the permission values (4+2+1=7). Read and execute permissions are a combination of 4+1=5. So, the three numbers you'll use to set this are 7, 5, and 5, entered as a single three digit number, 755. The syntax for this form of chmod is as follows: **chmod <permissions> <filename> <filename> ....**

For example, check out the following:

```
>chmod 755 magical-beans.gz
>ls -lg magical-beans.gz

-rwxr-xr-x 1 jray   test 1463882 Jul  2 11:33 magical-beans.gz
```

As you might hope, the owner has full read, write, and execute permissions, whereas the group and world have read and execute permissions. As you become experienced, you'll probably find that this second method is the fastest way to set permissions. Just remember read (4), write (2), and execute (1), and you'll be fine.

 Changing Permissions at the Directory Level   If you want to change the permissions of an entire directory structure (all the files and directories within a directory), you can use the commandline option -R with the chmod command to recursively change everything within a directory.

CHANGING A FILE'S OWNER: chown

This command isn't going to do you much good, because it can only be used by the super-user (*root*). If you need to change the owner of a file, ask your system administrator to run this for you. The syntax for chown is simple: chown *<new owner> <filename> <filename>* ....

For example, type the following:

```
>chown agroves magical-beans.gz
>ls -lg magical-beans.gz

-rwxr-xr-x 1 agroves test 1463882 Jul 2 11:33
➥magical-beans.gz
```

The file is now owned by the user agroves (as opposed to jray, who has owned it throughout this lesson).

 Another way to Grant Ownership   If, for some reason, another user needs to own a file that you own, you can always give them read permission and allow them to copy the file. The copy that is created is owned by the other user.

CHANGING A FILE'S GROUP: chgrp

Although you can't change a file's owner, you can change the group that a file belongs to with the chgrp command. To do this, however, you must be a member of that group. Your system administrator has the capability to create new groups and add users to these groups. If you have any questions about your own group membership(s), ask your administrator how your account was configured.

To use chgrp, follow these steps:

1. Choose the file or files you want to change.

2. Determine which group the file now belongs to.

3. Change the file's group using the following command: **chgrp**
   <new group> <filename> <filename> ....

For example, type the following:

```
>chgrp admins magical-beans.gz
>ls -lg magical-beans.gz

-rwxr-xr-x 1 agroves admins 1463882 Jul 2 11:33
➥magical-beans.gz
```

The infamous magical-beans.gz file now belongs to the group admins. Members of the group have read and execute permissions for the file.

The most obvious use for chgrp is if you are collaborating on a project. If you create a file that you want to share with many people, you'll need to change the group of the file to one that all the users belong to.

Running chgrp on a directory   The chgrp command, like chown, can also be run recursively on a directory by using the -R option. This is a big time-saver when you want to modify a bunch of files and directories at the same time.

LOGGING IN TO A NEW GROUP: newgrp

If you're working on a project, you might not want to constantly change the group of the files that you create; this might get pretty monotonous if you're working with hundreds of files. Luckily, there is a way to log in to a group that you are a member of. This is done by way of the newgrp command. All files that are created after executing this command are under the group membership to which you have switched. This change persists until you log out or use the newgrp command again. Use newgrp by typing the following: **newgrp** *<new group>*.

For example, type the following:

```
>newgrp admins
```

After this command is executed, all further files that are created in this session belong to the group admins.

Becoming Another User Temporarily: su

su, the substitute user command, enables you to switch to another user account from within a single login session. Under UNIX, this changes your *effective* user ID—which means that all files created will effectively be as if the other user created them. Your *actual* user ID remains the same, however. A noticeable side effect of this is that even though you've used su to "become" another user, running mail checks email for the user account that you initially used to log in. To use the su command, simply enter it as follows: su *<user to switch to>*.

For example, type the following:

```
>su agroves
Password: ******
```

If this were you, you might now use the whoami command as follows to verify that the system now believes that you are effectively agroves:

```
>whoami
agroves
```

Just as you had hoped! You can now perform operations under the agroves account.

Account Sharing Guidance   It isn't a good idea to share account passwords between users. For this example, you've seen a user switch to the agroves account, which isn't necessarily good. Because the system thinks the user is now agroves, most anything the user does is logged as being done by agroves—and she might not appreciate it very much.

A more proper use of su is to switch to *non-personal* accounts. There are several accounts that are owned by database servers and so on that are prime candidates for the appropriate use of su (to perform maintenance on the database files).

Because su has the potential for a significant amount of abuse, its use is frequently limited to users of administrative accounts, and in all cases uses of su are logged by the system. Experimenting with this command without permission will, at the very least, raise administrative eyebrows in your direction.

SUMMARY

In this lesson, you learned the purpose of permissions, owners, and groups. You now understand what is necessary to enable other users to access your files and how to collaborate on projects using group permissions. You might want to take a few minutes to talk to your system administrator to find out how he or she has decided to manage groups. Also, you might want to request that groups be created that include other users with whom you want to share files. Following is a look at some of the highlights from this lesson:

- **Permissions**—File permissions control who can access a file, and what level of access they have to a file. The three levels of permissions are read, write, and execute. These permissions can be applied to the owner, group, or world.

- **chmod**—The chmod command changes the permissions for a file or directory. There are two methods of operation—symbolic and numeric. They both accomplish the same thing, so use the one you feel comfortable with.

- **chown**—Only the super-user can change who owns a file. If you can convince your administrator to do so, chown changes the owner. Reasons why you might not want to try are covered in Lesson 20, "Privileged Commands."

- **chgrp**—You can change the group that a file belongs to with the chgrp function. You can only change the file to a group that you belong to.

- **newgrp**—Rather than constantly having to change the group for files you create, you can use newgrp to log in to a group of which you are a member. All files that are created for the remainder of your login session are created under that group.

- **su**—The substitute user command effectively switches to another user within a single login session. If you have the password of another account, you can use su to perform operations under this account. Any files you create are owned by this user.

Lesson 20

Privileged Commands

In this lesson you'll take a look at some of the special commands that UNIX users seldom encounter.

The commands in this lesson are restricted to being run by the root user, but the information here will help you understand some of root's concerns and help conversations with your system administrator to make a little more sense.

Because of the way that UNIX works (with multiple users, multiple processes, and files owned by potentially hundreds of people), there are certain commands which will cause chaos if entrusted to normal users. These commands do things such as format disks, reboot the system, and create or remove devices.

Single User Mode

Every UNIX machine can be configured to boot into *single user mode*, a mode where the machine has no network resources and can only support a single user logged in. This is a maintenance mode that enables the root user to repair problems with the system without having to worry about other users changing things that they are working on. With some versions of UNIX, if a machine experiences a particularly hard crash, it might reboot itself into single user mode automatically. Some require a root password before any commands can be entered, and others come up directly into a root shell. If you happen to crash a UNIX machine and it comes up in single user mode, DO NOT TOUCH ANYTHING! Anything you do has the potential to make diagnosing the crash impossible; worse, it can have devastating effects on the system. For the root user, a singe-keystroke typo in the rm command can delete the entire file system, from the top down.

fsck

Every now and then you might hear a system administrator grumbling about having to fsck a drive. UNIX tends to take reasonably good care of its drives, but problems do occasionally crop up. The fsck command is UNIX's disk fixer program, and it is used to clean up problems caused by crashes or errant pieces of software. Most UNIX systems fsck their drives on bootup, and the expected result is an analysis report containing the number of files and the fragmentation level of the drive. If you're watching a UNIX machine boot, do not be overly concerned if you see fsck report problems—UNIX automatically attempts to fix them. In most cases it will be successful, and after using fsck on the drives the system restarts the reboot process. If the drives have serious problems, the automatic fsck exits with the following error message: Run fsck by hand. If it does, don't touch anything—go find a system administrator.

mount/umount

The mount command tells the system to attach a disk drive to the file system at a particular directory. As discussed in Lesson 4, "The File System," UNIX abstracts the physical hardware by causing drives to appear as directories in the file system. This command tells the system how to access the drive or where to locate it on the network, and where to attach it to the file system. The umount command does exactly the opposite—it removes mounted devices.

If you log into the system and are greeted by a message that says something similar to No Home Directory - using /, don't panic. In all likelihood your home directory is fine—it's just on a drive that is not mounted. This doesn't happen often, but with drives and resources being shared over the network, it only takes one person tripping over a network patch-cable to make some devices unavailable until the wire can be repaired.

If you get the previously mentioned error, or are simply kicked right back off the system after entering your password (as happens with some systems), wait 15 minutes and try again before calling your system administrator. Chances are, they already know about the problem and are trying to fix it, but dozens of users calling to complain is slowing them down.

shutdown/reboot

Although personal computers are becoming increasingly picky about being shut-down instead of simply turned off, UNIX machines are still more picky. The difference, of course, goes back to the fact that UNIX uses dozens of cooperating programs to form what appears as the operating system. Each of these programs might be in the process of modifying, moving, creating, or deleting files at any point in time. If you simply shut off the power to a UNIX machine, you interrupt all these processes, and probably destroy any files they were working on at the time. If the files are simply things such as word processor documents, this is only a minor problem. Unfortunately, UNIX also moves around and updates files critical to the operating system. Simply shutting off the power to a UNIX machine has the potential to completely corrupt the drives, leaving the system unusable—in short, don't do it.

To prevent this problem, UNIX has a `shutdown` command and a `reboot` command, each with obvious goals. These two commands gracefully exit all running software, write out disk-cache information to the drives, and complete their respective tasks. They are restricted to the root user for obvious reasons, yet some UNIX hardware manufacturers have started putting soft-power switches on their machines. The soft-power switches don't actually turn the machine off; they execute the `shutdown` command, as root, without requiring a password. In the eyes of most system administrators, this is simply bad business. If your machine has one of these soft-power switches, please don't use it. Other users might be using your machine, or your machine might be providing disk resources to other machines. Shutting it down is likely to create havoc on your local network and earn you a high position on your system administrator's list of least favorite users.

chown

The `chown` command is used to change the owner of a file from one account to another. Obviously, a normal user can't use this command, but if you need this done, your system administrator can do it for you. Remember, you can always get a copy of a file that you can read by using the `cp` command—changing ownership might not be necessary.

Keeping Your System Administrator Happy

UNIX is a very literal operating system, and does more or less exactly what you tell it to do. If you end up doing something that damages your own account and need your system administrator to restore your account from a backup, expect him or her to be less than pleased. If you do something that causes a breach of network security or damages files belonging to other users on the system, expect him or her to turn into a fire-breathing ogre.

You're dealing with a class of professionals who have a very difficult job, and who have to balance the rigors of dealing with mind-warping technical problems, the composite needs of an entire user community, and the needs of individual users.

Most system administrators have the very best intentions and wishes for the user base they support, but they also are under severe time pressure. There are problem patches and security fixes that appear and need to be applied to the operating system on an almost daily basis—failure to apply any one can leave your system vulnerable to crashes or outside attack. There are the constant pressures from users who "absolutely need" to have something installed, or who just deleted the programming project that they have to demo next week. And, there are users who just need a hand understanding how something works.

Rarely do system administrators hear from users when things are going well, so it's not uncommon for them to become a bit user-shy. All these things add up to a workload that causes many system administrators to burn out in a very short period of time.

If your system administrator does a good job for you, keep the work that they do and what it means to you in mind when dealing with them. Saying "Thank you" every now and then can go a long way toward taming the fire breathing ogre, and rumor has it that Orange Crush or Mountain Dew and Pizza help, too.

SUMMARY

In this lesson, you were introduced to a few things that you shouldn't or
can't do in the hopes that understanding why you shouldn't and can't do
them will make your interaction with your system administrator easier.
System administrators have a hard job, and have to walk the fine line
between keeping the system functioning for all users (which sometimes
requires them to be hard-nosed and inflexible), and creating the environment the individual users need to work. Most are truly interested in making the system work the best that it possibly can for you, but many do not
have the time to have a lot of patience. Hopefully, an understanding of the
types of things that make your system administrator's life more difficult,
and why it is that you shouldn't do them, will enable you to stay on your
administrator's good side. Following is a review of some of the other
points from this lesson:

- Never touch a machine if it looks like its running a root shell.

- Don't bother root (your system administrator(s)) about
  unmounted drives, unless it's obvious that nobody knows
  about it.

- Never ever turn the power to your machine off without permission from your administrator. If you've got a shutdown button on
  your machine, pretend it doesn't even exist.

- Root (administrative users) can change ownership of files for
  you, but consider whether it's really necessary or whether a copy
  will do.

INDEX

graphical login, 10. *See also* login
  process
graphical user interfaces. *See* GUIs
greg command, 59-60
  -i option, 60
  regular expressions, 131
grep command, 140
groups
  changing, 186-187
  defined, 181
  logging in, 187-188
GUIs (graphical user interface), 26
  KDE (K Desktop
    Environment), 152-153
    compatibility, 35
    customizing, 162-163
    editor, 91-92
    *file management, 51-53,
      60-62*
    folders, 52
    help system, 23
    KZip tool, 109-110
    logging out, 12
    window features, 37
  X Windows, 26-27
    configuring, 30-31
    focused input, 29
    iconized windows, 30
    starting, 27-28
    three-button mouse, 29
    window managers, 32-34
gunzip command, 103
.gz filename extension, 81, 103
gzcat command, 103
gzip command, 103

H

h command
  less utility, 79
  more utility, 78
  vi utility, 86
-h option (built-in help), 20

-H option (enscript command), 170
hackers, 173
hard drives
  mounting, 40, 192
  removing, 192
hard links, 73
head command, 79-80
headers, printing, 170
Help menu commands, Contents, 23
--help option (built-in help), 20-21
help systems
  built-in help
    --help option, 20-21
    -? option, 20
    -h option, 20
  emacs editor, 90
  KDE (K Desktop Environment),
    23
  less utility, 79
  local documentation, 21-22
  manual pages
    defined, 16
    displaying, 17-19
    searching, 19-20
  more utility, 78
  newsgroups, 22
home directories, 42
HTML (Hypertext Markup
  Language) files, 81
.html filename extension, 81

I

-i option
  grep command, 60
  rm command, 67
I/O. *See* input/output
Iconify Window button (KDE), 37
iconized windows (X Windows), 30
icons (KDE), 37
if command, 145

Q-R

SAMS
Teach Yourself
in 10 Minutes

Quick steps for fast results™

Sams Teach Yourself in 10 Minutes *gets you the results you want—fast! Work through the 10-minute lessons and learn everything you need to know quickly and easily. It's the handiest resource for the information you're looking for.*

Sams Teach Yourself Linux in 10 Minutes

John Ray
ISBN: 0-672-31524-6
$12.99 US/$18.95 CAN
